W9-DDN-126

Sophocles'
OEDIPUS PLAYS
OEDIPUS THE KING,
OEDIPUS AT COLONUS,
& ANTIGONE

A CONTEMPORARY
LITERARY VIEWS BOOK

Edited and with an Introduction by
HAROLD BLOOM

Mount Laurel Library
100 Walt Whitman Avenue
Mt. Laurel, N.J. 08054-9539
(609) 234-7319

Aivedeson 16 95

© 1996 by Chelsea House Publishers, a division of Main Line Book Co.

Introduction © 1996 by Harold Bloom

All rights reserved. No part of this publication may be reproduced or transmitted in any form or by any means without the written permission of the publisher.

Printed and bound in the United States of America.

First Printing
1 3 5 7 9 8 6 4 2

Cover Illustration: Adaptation from an Attic red-figure vase depicting Oedipus and the Sphinx

Library of Congress Cataloging-in-Publication Data

Sophocles' Oedipus trilogy / edited and with an introduction by Harold Bloom.
p. cm – (Bloom's notes)
Includes bibliographical references and index.
Summary: Includes a brief biography of Sophocles, thematic and structural analysis of the work, critical views, and an index of themes and ideas.
ISBN 0-7910-4070-4. – ISBN 0-7910-4099-2 (pbk.)
1. Sophocles. Oedipus Rex. 2. Sophocles. Oedipus at Colonus. 3. Sophocles. Antigone. 4. Oedipus (Greek mythology) in literature. 5. Antigone (Greek mythology) in literature. 6. Greek drama (Tragedy)— History and criticism. [1. Sophocles. Oedipus Rex. 2. Sophocles. Oedipus at Colonus. 3. Sophocles. Antigone. 4. Greek drama—History and criticism.] I. Bloom, Harold. II. Series.
PA4417.S693 1995
882'.01—dc20
95-43496
CIP
AC

Chelsea House Publishers
1974 Sproul Road, Suite 400
P.O. Box 914
Broomall, PA 19008-0914

Contents

User's Guide

This volume is designed to present biographical, critical, and bibliographical information on Sophocles and the Oedipus plays (*Oedipus the King, Oedipus at Colonus,* and *Antigone*). Following Harold Bloom's introduction, there appears a detailed biography of the author, discussing the major events in his life and his important literary works. Then follows a thematic and structural analysis of the works, in which significant themes, patterns, and motifs are traced. An annotated list of characters supplies brief information on the chief characters in the works.

A selection of critical extracts, derived from previously published material by leading critics, then follows. The extracts consist of such things as early notices of the work and later evaluations down to the present day. The items are arranged chronologically by date of first publication. A bibliography of Sophocles (including important editions of his plays from the invention of printing to the present day, as well as selected English translations), a list of additional books and articles on him and on the Oedipus plays, and an index of themes conclude the volume.

Harold Bloom is Sterling Professor of the Humanities at Yale University and Henry W. and Albert A. Berg Professor of English at the New York University Graduate School. He is the author of twenty books and the editor of more than thirty anthologies of literature and literary criticism.

Professor Bloom's works include *Shelley's Mythmaking* (1959), *The Visionary Company* (1961), *Blake's Apocalypse* (1963), *Yeats* (1970), *A Map of Misreading* (1975), *Kabbalah and Criticism* (1975), and *Agon: Towards a Theory of Revisionism* (1982). *The Anxiety of Influence* (1973) sets forth Professor Bloom's provocative theory of the literary relationships between the great writers and their predecessors. His most recent books are *The American Religion* (1992) and *The Western Canon* (1994).

Professor Bloom earned his Ph.D. from Yale University in 1955 and has served on the Yale faculty since then. He is a 1985 MacArthur Foundation Award recipient and served as the Charles Eliot Norton Professor of Poetry at Harvard University in 1987–88. He is currently the editor of the Chelsea House series Major Literary Characters and Modern Critical Views, and other Chelsea House series in literary criticism.

Introduction

HAROLD BLOOM

Because of Freud's unfortunate formulation of "the Oedipus complex," we find it difficult to interpret the Oedipus plays of Sophocles without indulging in rather irrelevant Freudian considerations. Freud should have named it "the Hamlet complex," since that is what he suffered from, an accurate sense that "the poets" (meaning Shakespeare) had been there before him. In this case, Sophocles had not been there before him, since Oedipus in fact had no desire whatsoever, conscious or "unconscious," to kill his father and marry his mother. Once we clear that confusion away, at least we can confront the authentic difficulties presented by Sophocles' three extraordinary dramas.

They are three very different plays, and do not always illuminate one another. *Antigone* was first acted when Sophocles was around fifty-four years old; it is a mature and powerful tragedy, and is very much Antigone's own tragedy. *Oedipus the King* was first produced perhaps fifteen years later, and was regarded by Aristotle as the exemplary tragedy. Sophocles lived another twenty years, dying in 406 or 405 B.C.E., at the age of ninety or so. It is generally assumed that *Oedipus at Colonus* was the work of his final years, since its first staging was posthumous, about five years after the poet's death. The play, highly original and difficult, has a subtle relationship to the initial drama of Oedipus, and makes us read *Oedipus the King* differently, whether that is wholly valid or not. All three plays abound in ambiguities, pragmatically in ironies, but the irony or ambiguous wordplay of any one of them is not at all that of the other two.

Antigone, the Hegelian model of "a struggle between right and right," Antigone and Creon, turns upon the irony that Antigone's sense of "the law" relates to the gods, and Creon's to the state. Creon's stance is not intrinsically false, but it violates human dignity, and becomes something ugly because it is not appropriate to the human moment, as Antigone's position certainly is. *Hubris,* the arrogance of power, is now permanently associated with Creon's name, even as the courageous stubbornness of principle is Antigone's legacy.

But there are no qualities or principles most of us are prepared to associate unambiguously with the name of Oedipus, in either of the Sophoclean plays that feature him in their titles. Once we have set aside the irrelevant Freudian reductions, *Oedipus the King* becomes a battlefield of conflicting interpretations. Is Oedipus innocent, so that only the gods are culpable? Are we to prefer Oedipus or the Sophoclean gods? Is Oedipus to blame for being so intelligent that he destroys the illusions without which we cannot go on living? Or is fate alone guilty, however we judge the flaws of Oedipus and the gods? Are *all* notions of guilt or innocence of little interest to Sophocles, and does he care only for the strife between illusion and truth? Or are all these questions useless, because the language of Sophocles knows only ambiguity, at least in human terms? Shall we say finally that we can make no sense of Oedipus as long as he is alive, because his only authentic language is the language of the gods, who urge him to stop tarrying and to come join them as yet another oracular god, at the close of *Oedipus at Colonus*?

All of these interpretations have been subtly urged by distinguished, scholarly critics of Sophocles, and they cannot all be right, because they strongly contradict one another. *Hamartia,* Aristotle's tragic flaw, seems dubious when we apply it to Sophocles' Oedipus, who never aims inaccurately, and who seems to me absolutely guiltless, and horribly unlucky, that last phrase being quite ludicrous in the context of his terrible story. I do not think that Sophocles means to honor the gods, since clearly we are to prefer Oedipus to the gods. When Oedipus blinds himself, a Freudian tends to speak of symbolic castration, but I think that Oedipus is making a religious protest against Apollo, and so against the light that does not let us see. And yet the power and self-confidence of Oedipus, his proper faith in his own intellect—these are gifts of Apollo. Oedipus knows this, and so I interpret him as crying out against the nature of truth, since the truth can only drive you mad.

That is a very dark reading, and I would not assert that it applies also to *Oedipus at Colonus,* an uncanny work, resembling nothing else that I have read. Why are the gods not insane, since they know the truth? Oedipus, becoming a god, abandons his characteristic fur: Henceforth he will share in the anger of the gods, which evidently is very different from our own. Presumably the madness of the gods also has nothing in common with our own. Whatever it is that destroys us can have no effect upon them. A Bible-educated culture cannot fully understand *Oedipus at Colonus.* We begin to gain entrance into the play only when we apprehend that it is totally *other* from any idea of religion that we possess. ✣

Biography of Sophocles

Sophocles was born at Colonus, near Athens, Greece, around the year 496 B.C.E. The son of a wealthy family, he received a good education and distinguished himself in music (which he studied with the famous teacher Lamprus) and athletics. Because of his talent, good looks, and well-liked personality, he was selected to lead the chorus celebrating the victory over the Persians at Salamis in 480.

As an adult, Sophocles turned his energies to composing songs, paeans, and tragedies. When he was twenty-eight years old, he won first place in an Athenian dramatic contest, beating the legendary Aeschylus. Over the course of his life, he garnered more than twenty first prizes and never placed lower than second place, despite challenging competition from both Aeschylus and Euripides. Sophocles produced a great quantity of this high-quality work, writing an estimated 123 plays.

In addition to his prolific writing career, Sophocles faithfully performed his civic duties as a public servant. He worked in one or more foreign embassies and likely joined the board of treasurers of the Athenian League in 443–442. In the Samian War (440–439), he was appointed general and served with Pericles; he may have been a general on two other occasions as well, including the Peloponnesian War. He also allegedly founded a shrine of Heracles and performed as a priest of a minor healing god (Halon or Alcon) connected with the god Asclepius. After the failed Athenian attack on Syracuse in 413, Sophocles was designated one of ten respected counselors for the temporary guidance of Athenian affairs.

Ironically, the man who created some of the stage's greatest tragedies lived a remarkably happy life himself. Besides winning numerous prizes, Sophocles enjoyed widespread public popularity. Nicknamed the "Attic Bee" for his purported ability to draw sweet honey from words, he received many accolades and socialized with such luminaries as the historian Herodotus, to whom he wrote a poem (nonextant) around

441. The devoted Greek citizen and acclaimed artist continued writing until his death at the age of ninety in 406 B.C.E.

Sophocles introduced several ground-breaking elements in his dramas. Aristotle claimed that he pioneered the use of scene painting on stage. Sophocles also broadened the theatrical possibilities and allowed more complexity in drama by adding a third actor to Aeschylus' traditional pair. While he increased the Greek chorus from twelve to fifteen, he decreased its role and more fully integrated it into the action.

Sophocles branched off the most from his predecessor Aeschylus by discarding the trilogy format. Instead of writing three interdependent works suffused with a sense of divine will, Sophocles composed individual works that could stand on their own artistically. In doing so, he crafted plots with great economy and emphasized the human character in a time of trial. Rather than focus on the cosmic order, he explored the complicated ways in which the human will, along with human flaws such as pride and ignorance, interact with the incomprehensible forces of fate.

Only seven of Sophocles' plays and a fragment of another, *Ichneutae,* have been preserved. *Ajax* is considered the earliest surviving work, dating anywhere from 465 to 450. In the play, Sophocles adds new depth to familiar characters. Ajax attempts to kill his rival Odysseus and the two kings who support him but becomes distraught when he realizes what he has done. He debates suicide in an artfully crafted monologue and then shockingly kills himself on stage. The play ends with Odysseus finally convincing Agamemnon to allow Ajax an honorable burial.

Antigone, produced in 442 or 441, also concerns the social and emotional issues around death and burial. The heroine tries to bury her brother Polyneices, a traitor to Thebes, in defiance of King Creon. The king first decrees a sentence of death, then lessens it to life imprisonment. Before he can completely relent, however, Antigone kills herself. In their anger and sorrow, Creon's son—who was engaged to Antigone—and Creon's wife both commit suicide. The tragedy thus highlights the conflict between family ties and social edicts, between religious obligations and political decrees.

Trachiniae (The Trachinian Women) (c. 430–420) is Sophocles' only extant work to deal with the passionate love between a man and woman. Upon learning of her husband Heracles' infidelity, Deianira sends him a robe from the centaur Nessus that she believes will recapture his love. Nessus, who had been killed by Heracles, had tricked her; a substance on the robe kills Heracles and Deianira kills herself in grief and guilt.

Sophocles' most famous tragedy, *Oedipus Tyrannos* (also known by its Latin title, *Oedipus Rex*, and in English as *Oedipus the King*), debuted around 429. As the play unfolds, Oedipus learns the horrifying truth that he had unwittingly killed his father and married his mother. His mother, Jocasta, commits suicide and Oedipus blinds himself and goes into exile. The masterful, gripping drama has remained deeply influential on both the arts and psychological theory.

Electra, produced between 420 and 413, portrays another royal family wracked by tragedy. Electra hates her mother, Clytemnestra, and seeks vengeance for her father's death. Her brother, Orestes, enters the palace through cunning and, after a joyful reunion with Electra, kills their mother and her lover, Aegisthus.

The final two surviving plays, *Philoctetes* (409) and *Oedipus Coloneus* (*Oedipus at Colonus*; produced posthumously in 402), both center around exiled heroes. Philoctetes was abandoned by the Greeks on their way to Troy, until they learned that they needed his weapon to win. After much deceit, Neoptolemus and Philoctetes are reconciled to their own natures and their mission in society. In *Oedipus at Colonus,* the blind hero is led to Colonus by his daughter Antigone. Recognizing that he has reached the place where he will die, Oedipus is filled with a renewed power and confidence. He blesses Athens, curses his feuding sons, and nobly goes off to die. Like his unforgettable, mythic characters, Sophocles himself has lived on centuries after his death.

Oedipus the King, Oedipus at Colonus, and *Antigone* are now grouped together as a trilogy, sometimes under the title *The Theban Plays,* although the long intervals between the writing of the plays indicate that Sophocles himself did not regard them as a formal trilogy. ✣

Thematic and Structural Analysis

Oedipus' story begins well before he was born, when his father, Laius, the rightful king of Thebes, brought a curse upon himself and his family by violating the trust of a host: Laius would one day have a son, the curse promised, but would die at his hands. How this curse is fulfilled is an important part of the Theban saga, a cluster of myths and history treating Laius' family and Theban ancestors as far back as Dionysus and Cadmus. This saga and others like it—such as the Trojan and Mycenean sagas—were well known to Athenians in the fifth century B.C.E. and provided much of the material for the ancient poets and playwrights whose work has survived. The tragedians in particular—Aeschylus, Sophocles, and Euripides—drew deeply on mythic saga for their plots, Sophocles writing three Theban plays: *Antigone* (about 441 B.C.E.); *Oedipus the King* (around 429); and *Oedipus at Colonus* (written around 406; produced 401).

In transforming myth to drama, the Greek tragedians were in an extraordinary position. Their audiences—as many as 17,000 at a time assembling in outdoor theaters at dawn to watch plays for several days each year—knew the myths well, but the stories were little more than sketches, so the playwrights had to flesh them out with details that might be intensely contemporary. Thus Sophocles' *Oedipus the King* opens with a scene of plague—at which the audience would no doubt shudder, remembering the deadly plague that had devastated Athens only a year or so before. The question-and-answer pattern of the three Theban plays likewise reflects the growth of analytical and legal thinking in Athens at the time. And the prospect of war between Athens and Thebes in *Oedipus at Colonus* probably refers to the actual conflict between those cities at the time of the play's production.

Unlike Aeschylus' plays of the Mycenean saga (*The Oresteia*), which were staged together and so formed a trilogy, Sophocles' Theban plays were written years apart and out of chronological order. Perhaps Sophocles kept returning to the

Oedipus story because he saw in it a flashpoint for the most compelling human issues—questions of identity, fate, consciousness, responsibility, religion, and state authority. These issues indeed filled the air of fifth-century Athens, when a developing democracy and the concepts of logic and individuality clashed with powerful religious and mythic traditions. Through the figures of Oedipus and his family, therefore, Sophocles' Theban plays, spanning nearly half a century, reflect his preoccupation with both universal and contemporary questions and how he and his society attempted to resolve them.

Oedipus the King

Pestilence ravages Thebes when the play begins, so that "no children are born" and life seems to be coming to an end. In Greek myth a miasma of this sort symbolizes the overturning of the conventional order of the world, often the result of a grave human crime. Thus in the opening scene (**lines 1–299**), Oedipus, the king of Thebes, "whom all men call the great," is beseeched for help by the city's children and elders as their savior. For years earlier, when Thebes suffered a similar plague under the cruel Sphinx, it was Oedipus who rescued the city by solving the monster's riddle, for which he was made king. Now Oedipus declares that he knows how Thebes suffers—that he in fact suffers on behalf of the city—and that he has already sent his brother-in-law and fellow ruler, Creon, to Apollo's oracle at Pytho to learn what can be done.

Creon returns with the news that a pollution "grown ingrained within the land" must be driven away, its source being the unpunished murder of the previous king, Laius, some years before. This explained, the drama's propelling force emerges: It is to be the resolution of a mystery. Likewise, its strongest narrative pattern will be the question-and-answer of interrogation. Like many modern detective stories, most of the play's actions took place in the past; the drama lies in the revelation of their meaning.

Immediately questioning Creon, Oedipus learns that Laius left Thebes years earlier on an embassy abroad and was never seen again. The only member of his company to return described a highway robbery in which all but he were killed. Oedipus suspects that the king's murder had been plotted within Thebes, but Creon replies that at the time it was impossible to investigate the matter: "The riddling Sphinx induced us to neglect mysterious crimes and rather seek solution of troubles at our feet"—the very pestilence from which Oedipus first rescued Thebes. He determines to solve the mystery as he solved the Sphinx's riddle and to punish the murderer, saying (with what will be terrible irony), "Whoever he was that killed the king may readily wish to dispatch me with his murderous hand." The first scene concludes with these promising resolutions, and all exit but the chorus of elders, who pray to Zeus, Athena, Ares, and other gods to help avert this plague. Thus the first scene is framed by entreaties for help, first addressed to Oedipus and now addressed to the gods themselves—ominously likening Oedipus to divinity.

To begin the search (**lines 300–511**), Oedipus calls for Teiresias, the prophet who, though blind, knows "things teachable and things not to be spoken, things of the heaven and earth-creeping things." Teiresias, however, will not speak of Laius' murder, lamenting his terrible knowledge. His refusal soon infuriates Oedipus, who rashly accuses Teiresias of complicity in the murder and says that the instigator must have been Creon. This in turn angers the prophet, who declares that Oedipus himself is the land's pollution. Outraged, the king accuses the old man of being "blind in mind and ears" as well as eyes, and when Teiresias retorts that these are "the very insults which everyone soon will heap upon" Oedipus, the play's reversals begin. For Teiresias, who cannot see, knows; and Oedipus, who can see, does not know. Before leaving, Teiresias delivers a prophecy about Oedipus that is nearly a riddle:

> He shall be proved a father and brother both
> to his own children in his house; to her
> that gave him birth, a son and husband both;
> a fellow sower in his father's bed
> with that same father that he murdered.

In the next scene (**lines 512–697**) Creon, who by now has heard of Oedipus' charges against him, confronts Oedipus; and Oedipus, far from withdrawing the charges, declares that Creon is "proved manifestly to be the murderer" of Laius and is guilty too of attempting to steal his crown. Although Creon argues that there is no proof and he has no reason to conspire—he is, he says, satisfied with his portion of the reign—Oedipus will not listen and says that Creon must be killed. Just in time, Jocasta, Oedipus' wife and Creon's sister, appears and rebukes the two for their quarrel. The chorus too begs Oedipus not to cast away Creon, "dishonored on an obscure conjecture," and under this twinned pressure the king relents.

Now (**lines 698–923**) Jocasta questions Oedipus, and when she learns of the role prophecy has played, she dismisses the problem, telling Oedipus of Laius' own prophesied fate "that he should die a victim at the hands of his own son." But this, she declares, simply never happened: Instead, the dangerous son was exposed at birth on a pathless hillside, his ankles pierced and bound; and Laius "was killed by foreign highway robbers at a place where three roads meet." She concludes, therefore, that no faith is to be placed in prophecy.

But ironically her very words shake Oedipus. For learning that Laius had been killed at a crossroads just before he himself reached Thebes, Oedipus says, "I have a deadly fear that the old seer had eyes." This moment thus presents a crossroads in the drama as well, what is sometimes called the peripeteia, or turning point. Although Oedipus will continue aggressively to question others, really he now questions himself.

Desperate for more information, Oedipus summons the man who had witnessed the murder, now a herdsman, and while they await him, Oedipus tells Jocasta his fears. He had grown up in Corinth, the son of King Polybus and Queen Merope—or so he thought until he heard gossip that he was in fact not their son. Disturbed, Oedipus traveled to the oracle of Pytho for the truth, but there instead he learned worse: "I was fated to lie with my mother . . . and be murderer of the father that begot me." Horrified, he would not return to his parents in Corinth but instead traveled toward Thebes. Before reaching the city, though, he encountered a small party with a carriage at a branching of the road. They argued for the right of way, and in the scuffle that ensued Oedipus killed them all. To his horror, therefore, Oedipus begins to see that he may indeed be Laius' murderer. He and Jocasta retreat inside the palace to await the herdsman, and the chorus sings anxiously that the gods' oracles are not proving true: The initial disorder of Thebes' plague now seems to encompass the cosmos.

Jocasta, however, who returns to the stage to pray for Oedipus, is more concerned about societal chaos than cosmic: "When we look to him we are all afraid; he's pilot of our ship and he is frightened." The conflict has thus reached the point that either the gods are wrong, or the king is wrong, and both options are disastrous.

But suddenly (**lines 924–1221**) a messenger arrives from Corinth with the news that old Polybus is dead, and Jocasta and Oedipus at once take this as further proof against the gods' oracles—for clearly Oedipus did not kill Polybus, as foretold. Still, however, he fears the other part of his prophecy: that he will share his mother's bed. This too Jocasta now dismisses: "Before this," she says, "in dreams too, as well as oracles, many a man has lain with his own mother." The messenger tries to dissolve Oedipus' fears by revealing that in fact he was not Polybus and Merope's child. As a tiny baby Oedipus had been left "on Cithaeron's slopes in the twisting thickets" with the tendons of his feet pierced and fettered—from which he had acquired his name, for *Oedipus* can mean swollen-foot. The messenger himself had been given the baby by a herdsman "called Laius' man"—the very one being awaited.

At this revelation Jocasta begins to panic and urges Oedipus to pursue the mystery of his birth no further. But Oedipus, suspecting that she fears he will be revealed a slave, mocks her and presses on. In despair, Jocasta begs the gods to keep Oedipus from the knowledge of who he is and rushes from the stage. As they continue to wait for the herdsman, Oedipus muses that he may be the child of "beneficent Fortune"; and the chorus, that he may be the child of nymphs or even gods.

Finally the herdsman arrives. But when he realizes the nature of the investigation, he is terrified and will not answer questions until tortured. Miserably he admits that he gave the other man the baby, which he himself had received from Jocasta to expose. The pieces now together, Oedipus at last sees the terrible origins and meaning of his life. For far from untangling a simple mystery, he has found himself, as his father's killer and his mother's lover, to have unconsciously torn and twisted the most mysterious, inviolate human bonds. Screaming at his curse, Oedipus rushes inside the palace.

But the tragedy is not complete, for now (**lines 1222–96**) another messenger appears from within the palace with news: Jocasta has killed herself. He describes to the chorus how she ran raging into her room and "cursed the bed in which she brought forth husband by her husband, children by her own child, an infamous double bond." Oedipus, he says, then stormed in and found Jocasta hanging. He tore the brooches from her dress and, shrieking that his eyes should never see the crime they had committed, struck them with the pins until "the bleeding eyeballs gushed and stained his beard— no sluggish oozing drops but a black rain and bloody hail poured down."

Now the palace doors are thrown open and Oedipus appears, a sight to make the chorus shudder (**lines 1297–1530**). For Oedipus, once so mighty but having seen and done what no man should, is now "the most accursed." When Creon arrives, Oedipus begs to be taken to Cithaeron, the wild mountain where he began his life, to end it; he entreats Creon to care for his young daughters, who, he weeps, are doomed. Oedipus is then led inside as the chorus somberly watches the departure of this man "who knew the famous riddle and was a man most masterful," now swallowed by "the breakers of misfortune." And so paradoxically Oedipus has indeed become his city's savior, by containing within him and then removing from his people's midst the most horrific, disruptive crimes imaginable, while proving the truth of the gods' oracles.

Oedipus at Colonus

The second play chronologically in the Oedipus cycle resumes his story twenty years after his terrible discovery and exile. He has been wandering as a blind beggar with his daughter, Antigone, and as the play begins (**lines 1–116**) the two reach a holy grove, "shady with vines and olive trees and laurel," and decide to rest. The fact that they are exhausted, seemingly at the end of their strength, suggests the conclusive tone of this play—indeed, Sophocles' last.

But no sooner have Oedipus and Antigone sat than a stranger appears and tells them they must leave, for they stand upon sacred ground: "Most dreadful are its divinities, most feared, daughters of darkness and mysterious earth," the Furies. Oedipus, however, recognizing in this description the place where he was prophesied to die, asks the stranger to summon the king of the region. Oedipus then reveals to his daughter that he had learned long ago from Apollo's oracle that he "should find home among the sacred Furies," and that, dying there, he would confer benefit on those who received him, a curse on those who exiled him.

Now Oedipus and Antigone hide as the chorus appears (**lines 117–323**), outraged that their "inviolate thicket" has been entered and determined to find the culprit. When he presents himself, however, and reluctantly identifies himself as the infamous Oedipus, they are even more horrified and try to expel him at once. It is only when Antigone intervenes, proclaiming, "You will never see in all the world a man whom God has let escape his destiny!" that they begin to soften. Oedipus takes this opportunity to defend himself in a powerful speech—the first of several. "I suffered those misdeeds more than I acted them," he claims; "How was I evil in myself?" He finishes by asserting that he may in fact now be "endowed with grace by those who are over Nature," and he bids the chorus save judgment until Theseus, the king of nearby Athens, arrives.

But before Theseus does so, another figure appears: Antigone's sister, Ismene (**lines 324–460**). Her arrival elicits from Oedipus a lament that his care has been all in the hands of his daughters, never his sons, Eteocles and Polyneices. These sons turn out indeed to be the cause of Ismene's presence: although they had originally preferred that Creon rule Thebes after their father's exile, later they feuded, and Eteocles drove away Polyneices, who now plans retaliation by storming Thebes with the aid of Argos. At this threat, Creon wants Oedipus to return to Thebes and in fact is now marching to retrieve him, for he too knows the prophecy Oedipus has mentioned: that the exile will bring victory to those who keep him. This hypocrisy infuriates Oedipus, who rages that he had indeed originally wanted to be exiled from Thebes but later had cooled his temper and wished to remain—only to be driven away then by Creon and his sons: "For lack of a little word from that fine pair out I went, like a beggar, to wander forever!" Full of pity now, the chorus (**lines 461–550**) advises Oedipus to perform a ritual to appease the grove's Furies and begs him in the meantime to tell his terrible story. He does, reluctantly and in fragments, but still he stresses his innocence in not knowing what he was doing.

At last Theseus arrives (**lines 551–727**) and, though somber, offers Oedipus sanctuary—as he too had once been an exile. But Oedipus tells the king that he in fact comes to give something, "and the gift is my own beaten self: no feast for the eyes; yet in me is a more lasting grace than beauty." He is especially anxious for sanctuary now, having learned of Creon's approach. When Theseus asks Oedipus whether his acceptance will provoke trouble with Thebes, Oedipus replies that, should trouble ever stir between Athens and Thebes (as it indeed did when the play was written), the Athenians' receiving Oedipus' body will in fact assure their preservation. Theseus therefore promises to grant Oedipus' wish, and the chorus, full of hope, sings of Athens' great virtues as the king departs.

However, as Antigone declares, these virtues are to be tested at once, for now Creon arrives with guards (**lines 728–886**). He appears to be struck with pity at the sight of ravaged Oedipus and begs the old man to return. But Oedipus is indignant and rails against Creon's playing "rascal's tricks in righteous speeches" and swears that he will never save Thebes for either son: "What my sons will have of my old kingdom is just so much room as they need to die in!"

Meeting this harsh response, Creon has Ismene and Antigone seized and carried off and is just laying hands on Oedipus himself when Theseus returns with guards (**lines 887–1043**). He at once sends men after the kidnappers and rebukes Creon, who in turn replies that he did not believe Athens willingly hosted the horrific Oedipus. Again Oedipus declares innocence in his famous crimes and laments that he must again speak of these unspeakable things. At this Theseus puts an end to speech and marches Creon after the kidnapped daughters. The chorus (**lines 1044–98**) narrates what must be occurring between the absconding Thebans and the pursuing Athenians—a typical means of presenting to the Greek audience material technically difficult to stage.

The chorus concludes its song to announce the young women's return (**lines 1099–1138**), but in the midst of the joyous reunion with their father Theseus informs him that someone has arrived wishing an audience (**lines 1139–1253**). This turns out to be Polyneices, recently returned from his war mission to Argos. Antigone persuades her grudging father that there can be no harm in hearing him. Like Creon, Polyneices (**lines 1254–1447**) expresses pity at his father's wretched appearance but is coldly received. He tries to enlist his father's help in his war upon Thebes, plainly stating that with Oedipus' blessing he shall come to power. But Oedipus is adamant, citing his son's disloyalty years earlier and finishing with a curse: "You shall die by your own brother's hand, and you shall kill the brother who banished you." Polyneices is desolate but, despite Antigone's desperate entreaties, realizes that he "must go silently to meet this doom." Before leaving, however, he begs his sisters, once he is dead, to honor him with a grave.

Suddenly (**lines 1448–99**) there are tremendous explosions of thunder and lightning and Oedipus calls for Theseus: "God's beating thunder," he says, "any moment now, will clap me underground." Oedipus grows frantic that Theseus will not arrive in time to receive the blessing he must impart before dying, the chorus too clamors for the king's arrival, and at last Theseus appears (**lines 1500–1578**). Oedipus hurriedly explains to Theseus that he recognizes this tempest as part of the old oracle of his life and death: "I'll lead you to the place where I must die; but you must never tell it to any man . . . and this will count more for you than many shields and many neighbors' spears." No sooner does he speak than "the angel of the dead, Hermes, and veiled Persephone" appear to lead him on, and blind Oedipus himself leads his children and Theseus away. Waiting behind, the chorus prays that Oedipus will finally find peace.

Soon (**lines 1579–1669**) a messenger returns to announce that Oedipus indeed "has left this world." Having washed and wept with his daughters, he then was bid by an unearthly voice to go on. With only Theseus, Oedipus then entered the sacred zone. And, the messenger tells the chorus, when the others returned a moment later, Oedipus was gone and Theseus stood with "his hands before his face, shading his eyes as if from something awful, fearful and unendurable to see." Oedipus disappeared miraculously: "His end was wonderful if ever mortal's was"—and indeed his life was marked throughout by the sight of what is fearful to see.

His daughters, however (**lines 1670–1750**), are wretched, seeing no future and no refuge for themselves; they are as doomed as Oedipus had earlier described them. But Theseus (**lines 1751–1779**), telling them that "those to whom the night of earth gives benediction should not be mourned," persuades them to cease their crying and return to Thebes, where they may try to stop the war between their brothers. Thus the play concludes with an end of mourning, the hope of peace, and the transformation of Oedipus from the most reviled and cursed mortal to a blessing.

Antigone

The last in the narrative sequence of plays but the first written, *Antigone* is regarded by some critics as an embryonic expression of one of Sophocles' later themes, the dilemma of a character who believes he acts properly but breaks divine law through ignorance. Here the conflict focuses upon Creon, who appears in each of the three plays but whose character and role change to suit each conflict. The setting is Thebes just after the death not only of Oedipus but of his warring sons, Eteocles and Polyneices, "two brothers who died on one day by a double blow," having killed each other. Compounding the loss for the surviving sisters, Antigone in particular, is the new king Creon's edict that Polyneices may not be properly buried but left "unwept, untombed, a rich sweet sight for the hungry birds' beholding." Yet not to bury and mourn a kinsman is a terrible crime with eternal implications, so though her sister shies away, Antigone resolves to do it. Thus the play's opening conflict is between Creon and Antigone, between his mandated law and what she believes is a higher law. Antigone's resolution introduces another theme, however, which develops throughout the play: Acknowledging that she risks death in performing the burial, that she in fact prefers "to lie with [the corpse]," Antigone willfully mixes the living with the dead. This creates an atmo-sphere much like that at the opening of *Oedipus the King:* the perversion of the natural order.

As Antigone forms her resolve and spurns her more timid sister, Ismene **(lines 1–99),** the chorus enters and sings vividly of the recent war between the two brothers **(lines 100–162).** They are quickly followed by Creon **(lines 163–331),** who now broadcasts his edict: Because he considers anyone who threat-ens his state's well-being the worst of all men, and because Polyneices, in attacking Thebes for the crown, has done that, Creon decrees that Polyneices is an enemy of the state and is not to be buried. His body is being carefully guarded—but not, it turns out, carefully enough, for a guard now enters with the news that "someone left the corpse just now, burial all accomplished."

The chorus' first thought is that the action was a god's, a sus-picion Creon angrily dismisses. Rather, he charges that one of his own enemies has bribed a guard to do it. Despite the guard's protestations, Creon says that he must find the doer or he will be tortured until he confesses. "How terrible," exclaims the poor guard (like Creon himself in *Oedipus the King*), "to guess, and guess at lies!" Both he and Creon depart as the cho-rus sings of the marvels of man at his most clever, and his odi-ousness when dishonorable **(lines 332–83).**

The guard soon returns with Antigone, however **(lines 384–525),** and explains to Creon that, after stripping Polyneices' corpse "back to slimy nakedness," he and the other guards waited in hiding. When Antigone appeared and saw her work undone, she "cried the sharp and shrill cry of a bitter bird which sees the nest bare where the young birds lay"— another instance of perversion, for Antigone, at the traditional age for marriage and children, tends not the young but the dead. When Creon questions Antigone she angrily declares that she knew his edict well but that "it was not Zeus who made that order"; she has instead chosen to abide by "the gods' unwritten and unfailing laws" and to honor her dead kin in the underworld. After arguing with her to no avail, Creon abruptly decrees that she may "go down there . . . and love the dead" then, and condemns her to death. But now Ismene (**lines 526–630**) introduces a complication, asking if Creon will dare to kill his own son's promised bride. "There are other furrows for his plough," Creon retorts, and the sisters are taken inside as the chorus laments the end of the family.

Creon's son, Haemon, now appears (**lines 631–780**) and seems to join his father in demanding obedience to the state. But he slyly suggests to Creon that in fact many citizens privately do not share this view and grieve for the girl, and he urges his father to consider yielding: "A man, though wise, should never be ashamed of learning more, and must unbend his mind." Creon is not ready for this, though, and after an escalating argument Haemon leaves, threatening that his father will never see him again. Creon angrily plans Antigone's death: She shall be left alive in a hollowed cave until she dies.

With the chorus singing of the deadly power of love (**lines 781–987**), Antigone is led away, taken "alive to the shore of the river underground"—continuing the family trait of twisting the natural order. But this image also likens Antigone to various classical heroes who travel alive to the underworld, such as Odysseus and Heracles. And she maintains, as she is led away, that she is indeed a heroine, having upheld the proper order by respecting divine law over political.

To confirm this assertion, Teiresias enters (**lines 988–1090**) and tells Creon that he is "balanced on a razor's edge," that a sickness is striking the state: "All of the altars of the town are choked with leavings of the dogs and birds; their feast was on that fated, fallen Polyneices." Like Haemon, Teiresias urges Creon to relent. But Creon only rages more, now accusing the old prophet of corruption, until at last in anger Teiresias tells Creon that soon he himself shall "give corpse for these corpses, child of your own loins."

> For you've confused the upper and lower worlds.
> You sent a life to settle in a tomb;
> you keep up here that which belongs below
> the corpse unburied, robbed of its release.

Shaken, Creon is now persuaded by the chorus to undo his actions, and he hurries off with attendants (**lines 1091–1151**).

Soon, however, in the presence of Creon's wife, Eurydice, a messenger returns with terrible news (**lines 1152–1256**). The group had hastened to burn and bury Polyneices' body and then rushed to the tomb—but before reaching it they heard Haemon's lamenting voice. In a panic, Creon ordered his followers to move away the stones, and entered to see Antigone "hanging by the neck, caught in a noose of her own linen veiling." Creon then begged his son to come out, but Haemon ran at his father with his sword and, missing his mark, instead chose to kill himself. He embraced Antigone as he died, gasping out "red blood on her white cheek." Eurydice hears this in silence and returns inside, anxiously followed by the messenger.

At this point Creon returns with his son's body (**lines 1257–1353**), lamenting and blaming himself. His tragedy is not yet over, though, for now the messenger returns with worse news: Eurydice too has killed herself, cursing Creon "as the killer of children." Creon, claiming that he is "nothing more than nothing now," begs to be sent away, released from his life that is "warped past cure." Somberly telling him that no mortal can escape his fate, the chorus concludes that "happiness depends on wisdom all the way." ❖

—Jane Shumate

(Above translations are David Grene's, Robert Fitzgerald's, and Elizabeth Wyckoff's, respectively.)

List of Characters

Oedipus is the mythical ruler of Thebes who, before his birth, was fated to kill his father and sleep with his mother. To thwart this prophecy, his parents, Laius and Jocasta, bound and pierced the infant's feet and left him to die of exposure. The prophecy, however, proves true as Oedipus, who was rescued without his parents' knowledge, returns years later to unconsciously fulfill his fate. The embodiment thereafter of the most intolerable human crimes, Oedipus blinds himself and lives as an exile, until finally his paradoxical fusion of innocence and venality imbues him with grace.

The Sphinx is the monster—part woman, part lion—that plagues Thebes until its riddle is solved: What travels on four feet at morning, on two at noon, and on three at evening? Only Oedipus, a wanderer to Thebes, is able to answer that it is a human, who first crawls, then walks, then leans on a cane. For solving the riddle, Oedipus is made king of Thebes and is forever identified with his mental agility. What he does not know, however, is how horrifyingly the riddle's three simple demarcations of human life are to figure in his own life: as first the exposed baby, then the unwittingly guilty and headstrong man, and finally the groping old exile.

Jocasta is both Oedipus' mother and, unknowingly, his wife. Having borne him with the terrible knowledge of his fate, she, with her husband, Laius, exposes the infant; she comes to have no faith in prophecies when she sees how easily (she believes) this one has been averted. When she discovers her horrible mistake, she curses the marriage bed that witnessed it and hangs herself.

Creon is Jocasta's brother and therefore both Oedipus' brother-in-law and uncle. He appears in all three of Sophocles' Theban plays, but his character, beyond his technical relation to the others, varies according to the needs of each drama: the falsely accused coruler in *Oedipus the King*; the hypocritical old emissary in *Oedipus at Colonus*; and the rash, righteous, belatedly repentant king in *Antigone*.

Laius, the earlier king of Thebes, is Oedipus' father and the husband of Jocasta. He brings upon himself the curse that he will be killed by his own son after he betrays the trust of a host by kidnapping that man's son. Although he takes measures to avoid the curse, it nevertheless is accomplished when Oedipus kills Laius unwittingly in a brawl.

Teiresias is a blind prophet who appears in many Greek tragedies, usually providing information understood or believed too late. In the Theban plays, Teiresias warns Oedipus that he himself may be the criminal he seeks, and worse; Teiresias also tells Creon that his punitive actions against Polyneices and Antigone are greater crimes than the ones they have themselves committed.

Polybus, the king of Corinth, adopts Oedipus as an infant and raises him as his own until Oedipus, afraid of his fated crimes against his parents, leaves what he believes to be his home.

Merope is the queen of Corinth, adoptive mother of Oedipus.

Antigone is the daughter of Jocasta and Oedipus, and therefore both Oedipus' sister and daughter. She accompanies and tends to Oedipus in exile; she also buries her condemned brother, Polyneices, thereby earning her own condemnation to death by Creon.

The Furies are terrifying spirits of blood vengeance; alternatively, they are spirits of kindness and forgiving. Their holy grove near Athens is therefore a suitable resting place for the aged exile Oedipus, who likewise embodies both horror and blessing.

Theseus, the king of Athens, offers sanctuary to the old exile Oedipus. In return his city is granted an enduring blessing.

Ismene, Antigone's sister, remains in Thebes while Antigone wanders with Oedipus; likewise she shies away from her sister's rebellious act of burying their condemned brother Polyneices.

Eteocles, the younger of Oedipus' sons, forces Polyneices out of Thebes and subsequently kills and is killed by his brother.

Polyneices, the elder of Oedipus' sons, travels to the holy grove at Colonus to beg his father's help in wresting the kingship of Thebes from Eteocles, but Oedipus angrily refuses.

Polyneices goes on to fight Eteocles and both are killed; Creon later prohibits Polyneices' burial.

Haemon is Creon's son and Antigone's betrothed. He sides with her when she defies Creon, however, and kills himself upon her suicide.

Eurydice, Creon's wife, kills herself when she learns that her son has done so, cursing her husband as "the killer of children." ✤

Critical Views

[Aristotle (384–322 B.C.E.) was one of the greatest philosophers of classical antiquity and an enormous influence upon Western thought in the Middle Ages and Renaissance. The *Poetics*—one of several of his treatises devoted to literature and rhetoric—survives only in a fragment; the section we have deals largely with the theory and practice of tragic drama, and it becomes clear that Aristotle based most of his remarks upon Sophocles' *Oedipus the King*, which he seems to have regarded as the prototypical tragedy. In this extract, after discussing how the *Oedipus* exemplifies some of the basic elements of tragedy, Aristotle notes that the play also is one of the great instances of the cathartic effects of pity and fear.]

Reversal of the Situation is a change by which the action veers round to its opposite, subject always to our rule of probability or necessity. Thus in the Oedipus, the messenger comes to cheer Oedipus and free him from his alarms about his mother, but by revealing who he is, he produces the opposite effect. ⟨. . .⟩

Recognition, as the name indicates, is a change from ignorance to knowledge, producing love or hate between the persons destined by the poet for good or bad fortune. The best form of recognition is coincident with a Reversal of the Situation, as in the Oedipus. ⟨. . .⟩

Fear and pity may be aroused by spectacular means; but they may also result from the inner structure of the piece, which is the better way, and indicates a superior poet. For the plot ought to be so constructed that, even without the aid of the eye, he who hears the tale told will thrill with horror and melt to pity at what takes place. This is the impression we should receive from hearing the story of the Oedipus.

> —Aristotle, *Poetics* (c. 350 B.C.E.), in *Aristotle's Theory of Poetry and Fine Art,* ed. and tr. S. H. Butcher (London: Macmillan, 4th ed. 1907), pp. 41, 49

CICERO ON *OEDIPUS AT COLONUS* AS THE PRODUCT OF SOPHOCLES' OLD AGE

[Marcus Tullius Cicero (106–43 B.C.E.) was one of the most distinguished Latin orators and philosophers of his time. In the following extract from his short essay, *De Senectute* (On Old Age), Cicero recounts the legend—not otherwise verified, but likely to be true—that Sophocles defended himself from charges of senility by writing *Oedipus at Colonus.*]

Old men retain their mental faculties, provided their interest and application continue; and this is true, not only of men in exalted public station, but likewise of those in the quiet of private life. Sophocles composed tragedies to extreme old age; and when, because of his absorption in literary work, he was thought to be neglecting his business affairs, his sons haled him into court in order to secure a verdict removing him from the control of his property on the ground of imbecility, under a law similar to ours, whereby it is customary to restrain heads of families from wasting their estates. Thereupon, it is said, the old man read to the jury his play, *Oedipus at Colonus,* which he had just written and was revising, and inquired: "Does that poem seem to you to be the work of an imbecile?" When he had finished he was acquitted by the verdict of the jury.

—Cicero, *De Senectute* (c. 44 B.C.E.), in *De Senectute, De Amicitia, De Divinatione,* ed. and tr. William Armistead Falconer (Cambridge, MA: Harvard University Press, 1923), p. 31

FRIEDRICH NIETZSCHE ON THE PARADOXES IN THE OEDIPUS STORY

[Friedrich Nietzsche (1844–1900), the celebrated German philosopher and author of *Thus Spake Zarathustra* (1883–92), *Beyond Good and Evil* (1886), and other works, began his career as a classical scholar. In this extract from his first major work, *The Birth of*

Tragedy (1872), Nietzsche stresses the paradoxes in Oedipus' story: His yearning to avoid sin leads to sin, and his frantic activity in *Oedipus the King* leads to his passivity in *Oedipus at Colonus*.]

Sophocles saw the most suffering character on the Greek stage, the unhappy Oedipus, as the noble man who is predestined for error and misery despite his wisdom, but who finally, through his terrible suffering, exerts a magical and beneficial power that continues to prevail after his death. The noble man does not sin, the profound poet wishes to tell us: through his actions every law, every natural order, the whole moral world can be destroyed, and through these actions a higher magic circle of effects is drawn, founding a new world on the ruins of the old, now destroyed. This is what the poet, in so far as he is also a religious thinker, wishes to say to us: as a poet, he first presents us with a wonderfully intricate legal knot which the judge slowly unravels, piece by piece, to his own ruin; such is the truly Hellenic delight in this dialectical unravelment that it casts a sense of triumphant cheerfulness over the whole work, and takes the sting from all the terrible premises of the plot. In *Oedipus at Colonus* we encounter this same cheerfulness, but elevated in a process of infinite transfiguration. The aged man, afflicted by an excess of misery, abandoned to every misfortune that comes his way as a passively *suffering* man, is confronted by a superterrestrial cheerfulness that descends from the gods, which suggests to us that the hero, through his passivity, has found his supreme activity, the effects of which will resonate far beyond his own life, while his conscious strivings in his former life led him only to passivity. Thus the legal knot of the Oedipus fable, which mortal eyes could not disentangle, is slowly unravelled—and the most profound human delight overcomes us at the sight of this divine counterpart of the dialectic.

If this explanation does justice to the poet, we may still ask whether it has exhausted the content of the myth: and here it becomes apparent that the whole vision of the poet is nothing but that light-image that healing nature holds up to us after we have glimpsed the abyss. Oedipus his father's murderer, his mother's husband, Oedipus who solved the riddle of the Sphinx! What can we learn from the cryptic trinity of these fateful deeds? There is an ancient folk belief, particularly prevalent in Persia, that a wise magus can be born only from incest: our immediate interpretation of this, with reference to Oedipus the riddle-solver and suitor of his own mother, is that for clairvoyant and magical powers to have broken the spell of the present and the future, the rigid law of individuation and the true magic of nature itself, the cause must have been a monstrous crime against nature—incest in this case; for how could nature be forced to offer up her secrets if not by being triumphantly resisted—by unnatural acts? I see this insight as quite clearly present in the terrible trinity that shapes Oedipus' fate: the man who solves the riddle of nature—of the dual-natured Sphinx— must also, as his father's murderer and his mother's lover, transgress the sacred codes of nature. Indeed, what the myth seems to whisper to us is that wisdom, and Dionysiac wisdom in particular, is an abominable crime against nature; that anyone who, through his knowledge, casts nature into the abyss of destruction, must himself experience the dissolution of nature. 'The blade of wisdom is turned against the wise; wisdom is a crime against nature': such are the awful sentences that the myth cries out to us. But like a beam of sunlight the Hellenic poet touches the sublime and terrible Memnon's Column of the myth, which suddenly begins to resound in Sophoclean melodies!

—Friedrich Nietzsche, The Birth of Tragedy (1872), tr. Shaun Whiteside (London: Penguin, 1993), pp. 46–48

E. S. SHUCKBURGH ON THE MORAL FOCUS OF *ANTIGONE*

[E. S. Shuckburgh (1843–1906), a renowned classical scholar, wrote *A Short History of the Greeks from the Earliest Times to B.C. 146* (1901) and *Augustus* (1903) and edited many classical texts. In this extract, Shuckburgh counters the view of some scholars that in the conflict between Creon and Antigone in *Antigone,* both sides are half right and half wrong; instead,

Sophocles means us to view Antigone's position as the morally proper one.]

The simplicity of the plot is due to the clearness with which two principles are opposed to each other. *Creon represents the duty of obeying the State's laws; Antigone, the duty of listening to the private conscience.* The definiteness and power with which the play puts the case on each side are conclusive proofs that the question had assumed a distinct shape before the poet's mind. It is the only instance in which a Greek play has for its central theme a practical problem of conduct, involving issues, moral and political, which might be discussed on similar grounds in any age and in any country of the world. Greek Tragedy, owing partly to the limitations which it placed on detail, was better suited than modern drama to raise such a question in a general form. The *Antigone,* indeed, raises the question in a form as nearly abstract as is compatible with the nature of drama. The case of Antigone is a thoroughly typical one for the private conscience, because the particular thing which she believes that she ought to do was, in itself, a thing which every Greek of that age recognised at a most sacred duty,—viz., to render burial rites to kinsfolk. This advantage was not devised by Sophocles; it came to him as part of the story which he was to dramatise; but it forms an additional reason for thinking that, when he dramatised that story in the precise manner which he has chosen, he had a consciously dialectical purpose. Such a purpose was wholly consistent, in this instance, with the artist's first aim,—to produce a work of art. It is because Creon and Antigone are so human that the controversy which they represent becomes so vivid.

But how did Sophocles intend us to view the result? What is the drift of the words at the end, which say that 'wisdom is the supreme part of happiness'? If this wisdom, or prudence, (τὸ φρονεῖν) means, generally, the observance of due limit, may not the suggested moral be that both the parties to the conflict were censurable? As Creon overstepped the due limit when, by his edict, he infringed the divine law, so Antigone also overstepped it when she defied the edict. The drama would thus be a conflict between two persons, each of whome defends an intrinsically sound principle, but defends it in a mistaken way; and both persons are therefore punished. This view, of which

Boeckh is the chief representative, has found several supporters. Among them is Hegel:—'In the view of the Eternal Justice, both were wrong, because they were one-sided, but at the same time both were right.'

Or does the poet rather intend us to feel that Antigone is wholly in the right,—*i.e.,* that nothing of which the human lawgiver could complain in her was of a moment's account beside the supreme duty which she was fulfilling;—and that Creon was wholly in the wrong,—*i.e.,* that the intrinsically sound maxims of government on which he relies lose all validity when opposed to the higher law which he was breaking? If that was the poet's meaning, then the 'wisdom' taught by the issue of the drama means the sense which duly subordinates human to divine law,—teaching that, if the two come into conflict, human law must yield.

A careful study of the play itself will suffice (I think) to show that the second of these two views is the true one. Sophocles has allowed Creon to put his case ably, and (in a measure from which an inferior artist might have shrunk) he has been content to make Antigone merely a nobly heroic woman, not a being exempt from human passion and human weakness; but none the less does he mean us to feel that, in this controversy, the right is wholly with her, and the wrong wholly with her judge.
—E. S. Shuckburgh, "Introduction," *The Antigone of Sophocles* (Cambridge: Cambridge University Press, 1902), pp. xviii–xix

T. B. L. WEBSTER ON SOPHOCLES' CONCEPTION OF THE GODS

[T. B. L. Webster (1905–1974), a British classical scholar who taught at Oxford, Victoria University in Manchester, and the University of London, is the author of *Art and Literature in Fourth Century Athens* (1956), *From Mycenae to Homer* (1958), and *Athenian Culture and Society* (1973). In this extract from his study of Sophocles, Webster discusses Sophocles' conception of the gods and its possible derivation from previous Greek thought.]

The gods administer justice in accordance with their laws. In the *Antigone* they are 'unwritten and sure laws of the gods not for yesterday or to-day, but eternal'; in the *Tyrannus* the chorus sing of laws which are 'set forth high footed, born in the heavenly aether, of which Olympus alone is father, nor did the mortal growth of men bear them, nor will forgetfulness ever put them to sleep'. They are partly moral commands such as 'bury the dead', 'avenge the dead', 'commit no injustice', and partly universal principles such as the danger of excess and the changes of human fortunes. For both there are analogies in other writers from the time of Hesiod onwards, and Sophocles is writing in a well-established tradition. Hesiod's Zeus appointed this law for men, that the beasts should eat each other but men should have justice. Empedocles, in phraseology which recalls the *Tyrannus,* says that 'the law of all (not to kill the living) is stretched through the wide ruling heaven and the unapproachable light'. The Aeschylean divine law, that the doer shall suffer and the sufferer learn, is rather a cosmological principle than a moral law. Similarly, for Heraclitus the law of god is the principle on which the universe works and 'to speak wisely a man must arm himself with it as a city with a law and much more strongly. For all human laws are nourished by the one divine law.' Sophocles is perhaps nearest in phrasing and idea to Heraclitus and Empedocles.

—T. B. L. Webster, *An Introduction to Sophocles* (London: Methuen, 1936), pp. 27–28

E. T. OWEN ON DRAMATIC TECHNIQUE IN *OEDIPUS THE KING*

[E. T. Owen (1882–1948) was a classical scholar who wrote *The Story of the Iliad, as Told in the Iliad* (1947). In this extract, Owen examines how Sophocles maintained dramatic tension in *Oedipus the King*, a play in which the outcome of the plot was probably known to his audience.]

The groundwork of Sophocles' plan is to tell, through one action that begins and completes itself before our eyes without pause or rest, the story of Oedipus from his birth to his fall. He does this by making that action how Oedipus discovered the secret of his birth. His task therefore was to invent the circumstances of the discovery, and make it from start to finish an apparently inevitable process, a process that once begun constantly supplies its own reason for its continuance; for this is the condition that creates the feeling of tension, which is the basis of dramatic enjoyment. Thus his first objective, so far as the machinery of the plot is concerned, was to contrive the mutual confessions of Jocasta and Oedipus, and the scenes with Teiresias and Creon are, mechanically, the means for attaining it. Teiresias is provoked to denounce Oedipus as the slayer of Laius: Oedipus, concluding, from this outrageous charge, that there is a plot between the prophet and Creon to oust him from the throne, quarrels with Creon, and Jocasta appears to part them; her inquiry into the cause of the trouble leads to her inadvertent dropping of the first clue. Looked at just in this way the play might be judged slow in getting to work. Neither Teiresias nor Creon contributes anything directly to the telling of the story; they merely create the occasion for it. Two long scenes (running to over three hundred lines) are taken up with what looks like a single step in the advancement of the action, the bringing about of the scene between Oedipus and Jocasta. But while the story must be told, a dramatist's chief concern is not that, but to give the audience a good time by his way of telling it, to give them the best time he can, and this involves all sorts of considerations over and above getting the necessary facts of the story before them. Dramatic construction lies there.

We must bear in mind that Sophocles builds his effects on the audience's presumed knowledge of the outcome. He has therefore constructed these early scenes also to get the most out of the ironic contrast between appearance and reality. For there is here the opportunity not only of progressively sharpening and deepening the "irony," but of prolonging suspense, keeping the audience breathlessly waiting for the expected blow to fall. It is the plain duty of an alert artist to exploit these possibilities to the uttermost.

—E. T. Owen, "Drama in Sophocles' *Oedipus Tyrannus*," *University of Toronto Quarterly* 10, No. 1 (October 1940): 49–50

C. M. BOWRA ON THE CONTRAST BETWEEN *OEDIPUS THE KING* AND *OEDIPUS AT COLONUS*

[C. M. Bowra (1898–1971) was a fellow of Wadham College, Oxford, and a prolific critic of ancient and modern literature. Among his books are *Tradition and Design in the* Iliad (1930), *The Greek Experience* (1957), and *Periclean Athens* (1971). In this extract from his monograph on Sophocles, Bowra dismisses any biographical considerations concerning *Oedipus at Colonus* and declares that, whereas *Oedipus the King* showed the power of the gods to humble human beings, *Oedipus at Colonus* shows the gods' power to exalt them.]

In 406–405 B.C. Sophocles died in his ninetieth year, and *Oedipus at Colonus* was produced by his grandson in 402. It has the peculiar interest that belongs to the last work of a great poet, especially since it was written in extreme old age and is in this respect comparable to the last dialogues of Plato or the last paintings of Titian. When Sophocles wrote it he must have known that the end was near, and it is only natural to assume that in it he took a kind of leave to his life and gave his conclusions on it, rather as Shakespeare is thought to have taken leave of the stage and dramatic poetry in *The Tempest*. It has in consequence often been treated as if it were a more personal and more intimate document than his other plays. Its episodes and emotions have been explained with reference to the poet's last years. The angry old man, Oedipus, who quarrels with his son, is compared with Sophocles who quarrelled with Iophon; the lament of the Chorus on the miseries of old age is sometimes thought to have little dramatic relevance and to be the old poet's lamentation on his private sorrows; even the hero-ization of Oedipus has been claimed to show prophetic insight into the destiny which awaited Sophocles after death. But such views, even when based on sufficient evidence, reveal nothing about the actual play. They may help to explain why Sophocles wrote the play or wrote it as he did, but not what the play is or what it means. They belong, if anywhere, to the poet's biography, not to the study of his work. Nor do they help us to understand the play. It stands in its own strength and needs no reference to such external facts. It is written with remarkable power and shows no signs of flagging inspiration. It has a noble and simple design. And more than any other Greek play it touches the heart of Greek religion with its belief in the existence of two worlds, natural and supernatural, human and divine, separate yet often interpenetrating, and at times united.

The central theme is the transformation of Oedipus into a hero. As such he seems to have been honoured in Sophocles' own deme of Colonus, and it is unlikely that Sophocles invented the whole story. It was no doubt of little importance, but in the last years of the fifth century devout and patriotic Athenians must have turned their minds to all the supernatural helpers that they could find. In this case they may have felt that the hero had proved his worth. For near Colonus the Athenian cavalry had defeated a Theban force in 407 B.C., and some may have attributed the victory to the dead hero who was hidden near the battle-field. Since Sophocles was familiar from childhood with the neighbourhood and its memories he may have been impressed by the event and seen in it a sign of the care which the gods had for Attica. In any case the theme of a hero in Attic soil permeates the play. The power of such a tutelary being is assumed and indirectly dramatized. This hero is the same person whose hideous misfortunes Sophocles had already presented in *King Oedipus.* His *Oedipus at Colonus* is in some senses a sequel to the earlier play. It shows how a lifetime of sufferings closes in peace and power; it displays the power of the gods to exalt, as *King Oedipus* displayed their power to humble; it shows that they who have seemed cruel and relentless can grant rewards and make amends. It concentrates on the heroization of Oedipus, and in this it differs from the *Phoenician Women* of Euripides which also dealt with Oedipus' old age and foretold his end at Colonus but said nothing about his becoming a hero (1703–7). Whatever Sophocles may owe to the play of Euripides, he does not owe to it his central formative idea. What concerns him is precisely Oedipus' heroization. In his old age, in the darkening shadows of a hopeless war, he turned his thoughts to the landscape of his own home and to its indwelling power. Just as he won his first prize in 468 B.C. with *Triptolemus* on an Athenian legend and an Athenian cult, so in his last play he dramatized another legend and honoured another cult from his own place. At a time when his country needed every possible help, he thought of the unseen helper in Colonus and made his heroization the subject of a play. ⟨. . .⟩

The paradox of *Oedipus at Colonus* is the transformation of the polluted, blind, poverty-stricken Oedipus into something more than man. This is the dramatic stuff of which it is made. We know that Oedipus has been in conflict with the gods because he has broken their laws; we soon hear that he is still in conflict with men. These conflicts are resolved in a final reconciliation when the gods take him to their own and his transformation helps his friends and harms his enemies. Even his old conflict with himself, his sense of uncleanness and degradation, is overcome. He learns that the gods do not hate but love him, that they wish not to humble but to exalt him. The chaos of his life, pierced by shame and hatred and contempt, is reduced to order. And this reversal is of much more than fortune. The play displays the beginning and the end of it, shows first the abject poverty of Oedipus and then the special attentions which the gods pay to him. The change from one state to the other is not sudden or abrupt. It takes place through the play. Oedipus discovers not only that he is destined for this high end, but gradually, without himself knowing it, he feels in himself the qualities of a hero, a *daimôn,* a being more powerful than men. He grows in strength and stature until he is able, blind though he is, to find his way unguided and unhelped. The divine power is at work in him to prepare him for what he is to be. The process of his transformation is highly dramatic. He is subjected to searching tests, and in each he shows his new strength, his more than human character. At the end he has found his new nature in all its force. He is ready to join the gods.

—C. M. Bowra, *Sophoclean Tragedy* (Oxford: Clarendon Press, 1944), pp. 307–8, 310

CEDRIC H. WHITMAN ON OEDIPUS' WISDOM, MISFORTUNE, AND GUILT

[Cedric H. Whitman (1916–1979) was Eliot Professor of Greek at Harvard University. He wrote *Homer and the Heroic Tradition* (1958), *Euripides and the Full Circle of Myth* (1974), *The Heroic Paradox* (1982), and other works. In this extract from *Sophocles: A Study of Heroic Humanism* (1951), Whitman comments on Oedipus' wisdom, misfortune, and guilt in *Oedipus the King*.]

Oedipus was proverbial for two things—sagacity and atrocious misfortune. Greek popular wisdom had it that if a man were careful and prudent, he would avoid trouble. Of all men, Oedipus should have succeeded, but of all men he particularly did not. Oedipus remains a type of human ability condemned to destruction by an external insufficiency in life itself—as if knowledge were possible, but the objects of knowledge, to use Plato's phrase, were somehow illusory, or at least evil. Such is Oedipus in the Sophoclean version, and such he must have been always. The myth is ultimately its own best interpreter and needs no *fabula docet.* It is for form's sake alone that the *Oedipus Rex* closes with the same old Herodotean saw which opened the *Trachiniae:*

> Let mortals hence be taught to look beyond
> The present time, nor dare to say, a man
> Is happy, till the last decisive hour
> Shall close his life without the taste of woe.

These closing lines have been thought to be the moral, but if this were all, there hardly needed to be any play, not to mention the chaotic masses of critical material which it has occasioned.

The *Oedipus Rex* passes almost universally for the greatest extant Greek play—an assumption based, no doubt, on Aristotle's preference. This judgment might perhaps be questioned since it does tend to thrust other monuments of the Greek theatre into the background and narrow our conception of what tragedy "should be." But it is more pertinent to ask how the *Oedipus* has sustained its reputation in view of the interpretations put upon it—particularly those interpretations which treat the play as a vivid proof of Sophocles' simple faith and pure piety.

⟨. . .⟩ *Oedipus Rex* is, by this time, buried under so many layers of critical acumen, that anyone who dares believe in the innocence of Oedipus must answer formidable philologists and prove his mettle. Indeed, to those who consider Oedipus morally guilty of parricide and incest, there is little that can be said, for of course he committed these crimes, however unwittingly. Although Aristotle, who distinguishes carefully between the willful act and the unconscious act, would surely disagree, it might be urged that Oedipus' crimes are more in the religious than the purely legal or moral context, and that therefore, whatever his motivating intention, Oedipus himself is just as "hateful to the gods"—in the eyes, at least, of the ancient chthonian religion, with its blood-for-blood law, defended and exalted by daemonic hosts of Furies, with their attendant spirits, the *Alastores* and *Miastores.* But although this old religious attitude may have still prevailed among most Greeks of the time, it is doubtful how far and how simply Sophocles could have believed in the shadowy bloodhounds of murder in the middle of the Periclean age of reason. In 458, the Athenian public had witnessed the trial scene of the *Eumenides,* and had seen Orestes acquitted in the final court of appeal; and if Orestes, why not Oedipus? But there was no orthodox creed in these matters. Even if the gods themselves were supposed to hold Oedipus guilty (and apparently they did), Sophocles was free to differ. In fact, it was the office of the tragic poet to hold his own values and to use these, not the plastic figures of the gods, as his moral standard. That perhaps is the crux of the problem: in popular belief the gods were supposed to hate and punish Oedipus for what he actually did; Sophocles, on the contrary, has painted him as a man willfully innocent, passionately honest in motive, and full of heroic arete. And if he did so, he must have thought so, and he could not have concurred with the judgment of the gods.

It is precisely this difference of opinion between the gods and the poet, corresponding as it does to the disproportionate disposal of sin and punishment in the myth, which has made it so hard to adjust the apparent piety of Sophocles to the unmitigated pessimism inherent in the action of the *Oedipus*. To try to reconcile these opposites and draw therefrom a salutary lesson in sophrosyne is likely to lead to self-contradiction. The gods cannot be just, if Oedipus is morally innocent. Yet, as the hero's character stands, this seems to be the case. The implications are so gloomy, and so different from the traditional picture of Sophocles, that it has been proposed that Sophocles must have had some compensating thought in mind, and that the play must be a treatise on either the nothingness of man, the necessity of religion, or sometimes both.

—Cedric H. Whitman, *Sophocles: A Study of Heroic Humanism* (Cambridge, MA: Harvard University Press, 1951), pp. 122–23, 128–29

RICHMOND Y. HATHORN ON EXISTENTIALISM IN *OEDIPUS THE KING*

[Richmond Y. Hathorn (b. 1917) is a former professor of classics and comparative literature at the State University of New York at Stony Brook. He is the author of *Tragedy, Myth, and Mystery* (1962) and *Crowell's Handbook of Classical Drama* (1967). In this extract, Hathorn shows that Oedipus' acknowledgment of his guilt is in tune with the existential nature of his crime.]

The person who wholly projects morality into the outer world loses his own selfhood in the process. Sophocles does not waste his time and the reader's patience by making Oedipus lament at the last that he could not help doing what he did or being what he is. To look upon oneself as the mere product of external causes is to make oneself a thing instead of a person, as the existentialist philosophers never tire of pointing out. Oedipus is horrified at having been his own self-accuser, but he does not therefore retract the accusation. He realizes that he is a scapegoat; he does not complain that he is a goat. Determinism, theories of heredity and environment, fatalism: all are devices, not for explaining guilt and evil, but for explaining them away, away from ourselves, at all costs; Oedipus disdains to avail himself of these devices. Rather he reaches his true moral stature at the end of the play. For a man is never more conscious of being a person and less conscious of being a thing than when the self is accusing itself and accepting its own guilt. The willingness to accept guilt is an indispensable step toward the goal of self-knowledge; an animal, a savage, or a child cannot fully grasp the concept of guilt; similarly an adult who falls into deterministic excuses for his behavior shuts the door on the possibility of self-development. But a person reaches his greatest intensity of self-consciousness when he simultaneously plays the part both of the accuser and the accused. To such intensity the individual will not rise as long as his external fortunes are in a condition of prosperity; herein lies the necessity of tragedy. Albert Camus remarks, "The human heart has a tiresome tendency to label as fate only what crushes it. But happiness likewise, in its way, is without reason, since it is inevitable. Modern man, however, takes the credit for it himself, when he doesn't fail to recognize it." Sophocles, needless to say, knew better than the "modern men" of his day.

Even the recognition of an unpleasant truth is a moral act; if a man is hideously ugly, he deserves some praise for taking an honest and steady look in the mirror. Morality is not a matter of putting some goodness or wickedness into a slot and receiving in return a proportionate package of pleasure or pain. *Oedipus Rex* is not a crime-and-punishment play; it is a moral drama of self-recognition. That the recognition is neither prompt nor willing is natural, and increases our feelings of pity and fear.

The view that represents Sophocles as an advocate of mere religious conventionality and ethical conformity is inadequate. Oedipus as a scapegoat is singled out, but, by accepting the role, he singles himself out and differentiates himself from the mass, the Chorus. His acceptance of the wretched creature that he is makes him a hero. His life is henceforth to be unique, a life set apart, as he well recognizes, and in this respect it is to become the being of a Person in contrast to the existence of a Thing. But the Chorus are quite willing to dissociate themselves from him and to withdraw into the anonymity of convention, a withdrawal which, as Heidegger repeatedly emphasizes, is one of the chief methods of evading human freedom. The Chorus say that they take Oedipus as their *parádeigma,* their model from whom they may learn a lesson, but their wish never to have known him shows that his is a lesson that they are not actually prepared to learn. Thus they fall into the same error from which Oedipus is emerging.

It is ambiguous, therefore, to say that Sophocles does not offer a solution to the problem of evil such as Aeschylus gives. This is usually taken to imply an attitude of pessimism on his part, at worst marked by befuddlement or bitterness, at best stoical or pietistic. But, after all, evil by definition is that to which there is no ultimate solution. It is a mystery, for even exterior evil always has inextricable connections with the self. Any evil outside myself, once acknowledged, immediately offers an ineluctable challenge to me; if I refuse to act or react—and strictly speaking I can only apparently refuse—I compound it. And interior evil, the evil of my own limited destiny, is the precondition of my action or reaction. Let it be said again that Oedipus' prime *hamartia,* his blind spot, his moral ignorance, is precisely his tendency to suppose that evil is a problem rather than a mystery, a something exterior to the self that can be solved without involving the self.

—Richmond Y. Hathorn, "The Existential Oedipus," *Classical Journal* 53, No. 5 (February 1958): 226–27

G. M. Kirkwood on Antigone and Ismene

[G. M. Kirkwood (b. 1916) is the Fredric I. Whiton Professor of Classics at Cornell University. Among his many books are *Early Greek Monody* (1974), *Selections from Pindar* (1982), and *A Study of Sophoclean Drama* (1958), from which the following extract is taken. Here, Kirkwood notes the extreme contrast in temperament between Antigone and her sister Ismene in *Antigone*.]

Antigone and Ismene are together in two scenes, in the prologue and at the end of the second episode. The contrast between them is not that of devotion to a cause *vs.* timidity; it is more complex than that and more revealing of the character of Antigone. Of course Antigone is devoted and has a cause; and Ismene, by contrast, is timid. But to what, exactly, is Antigone's devotion, and what does it indicate about her? The contrast with Ismene helps us to answer these questions. In the prologue Antigone's first concern is not for religious duty, which looms so large in her scene with Creon. Her first reaction is a personal one; the matter is one of family loyalty, where, she feels, Creon has no right to intrude. Antigone is intense, as we see from the opening line on; her greeting to Ismene has more of intimacy and passion than of loving gentleness. To Creon's clumsy interference with her duty to her family, she responds with instinctive hostility. She is furious that Creon should seek to legislate to her in a matter so personal to her: "Such conditions they say the worthy Creon has proclaimed for you and me—yes, even for me" (32–33)! The burial of Polyneices becomes for her the very touchstone of nobility, and she declares that Ismene by her attitude toward it will show "Whether you are of noble nature (εἴτ' εὐγενὴς πέφυκας) or base though your parents were good" (38). Like Ajax and Deianeira, Antigone has an unhesitating devotion to her concept of what is becoming to the εὐγενής.

In all this there is no thought of the ἄγραπτα νόμιμα ⟨unwritten laws⟩; up to this point Antigone has not reflected and has not formulated her instinctive idealism. She is not to be thought of as primarily a philosopher or an embodiment of the reasoned way of life. By the contrasting reaction of Ismene we understand more clearly what Antigone is. Ismene's conduct is equally instinctive. Suddenly confronted with a bold and illegal scheme, she shrinks at once, for her instinct is to obey, just as surely as Antigone's is to exercise her own will: she is a woman, and cannot fight against men (61–62); she must obey (47, 59, 79); Antigone's plan lacks common sense (68); those below will forgive her for not acting (65–66); she cannot act βίᾳ πολιτῶν ⟨in defiance of the state⟩ (79). So far as moral attitude is concerned, there is no fundamental difference; Ismene is as aware as Antigone of the wrongness of Creon's edict. The difference is in personality: Ismene is without the imperiousness, willfulness, and single-mindedness of her sister; she is prudent and sees other aspects of the situation. Antigone has eyes for only the one issue that is to her all-important.

There is another contrast between them. When Ismene shows reluctance to act, Antigone becomes instantly hostile. She declares bitterly that she would not now accept her sister's help if it were offered (69–70); when Ismene advises silence and says that she too will be silent about the plan to bury Polyneices, Antigone angrily bids her tell it to all (84–87). Antigone promises Ismene the hatred of their dead brother and of herself (93–94); Ismene in the last words of the prologue assures Antigone of her love, mad though she may be. It is Ismene, then, who has something like the gentleness and affection and patience that we have seen in Tecmessa and Deianeira; relatively, Antigone is hard, abrupt, intolerant, and in this she is like Ajax. It is the natural concomitant and price of her firmness and single-mindedness.

The second incident continues the contrast. To Ismene's unexpected and courageous attempt to assume joint responsibility for the burial and to share the punishment, Antigone's response is a passionate rejection. Both reactions are, superficially, strange; but both are in place. We soon learn Ismene's reason: so warmly does she love her sister that she cannot face life without her (548), and this is what inspires her with courage. Antigone's conduct is a continuation of what we saw in the prologue. The harshness with which she here spurns Ismene is no different from her impetuous scorn there. Antigone knows that Ismene is even yet not in real sympathy with her spirit. For Ismene is acting out of affection; Antigone's drive comes instead from her concept, at first intuitive, now formulated, of noble conduct.

—G. M. Kirkwood, *A Study of Sophoclean Drama* (Ithaca, NY: Cornell University Press, 1958), pp. 119–21

H. D. F. KITTO ON THE ROLE OF THE GODS IN *ANTIGONE*

[H. D. F. Kitto (1897–1982) was a professor of Greek at the University of Bristol, England, and a well-known classical scholar. Among his publications are *Form and Meaning in Drama* (1956), *The Greeks* (1957), and *Greek Tragedy: A Literary Study* (1966). In this extract, Kitto declares that the role of the gods is crucial to the understanding of *Antigone,* both in the conflict between Antigone and Creon and between Creon and Haemon.]

Mr. F. L. Lucas has recently declared his opinion that the final scenes of the *Antigone* are weak: the play flags when Antigone is removed. Mr. Lucas is by no means the first critic to say this. The criticism proves one thing conclusively, that the critic has not understood what the play is about. On the one level Mr. Lucas has understood the play well enough, that on which the heroic and passionate Antigone defies the tyrant at the cost of her life. On this level the gods do indeed come into the picture, since Antigone is convinced that she is doing the gods' will. But this is only part of the picture, and if one sees only a part, under the impression that one is seeing the whole, it is not surprising if one finds the picture ill-designed. Mr. Lucas and those who agree with him think that the *Antigone,* like other Greek plays, is concerned with exciting or at least interesting people and actions—as of course it *is*—and when the most exciting one disappears from the action he begins to yawn. What the critic is really yawning about is the gods; he does not realize that they are there, and have been from the beginning. They enter into the structure of this play more than some of us realize.

I will begin with Haemon's exit. He came in to plead with Creon for Antigone's life, and has been so brutally repulsed that he has gone out making obscure threats towards his father. At this point the chorus performs an ode, a typical choral ode, filling a pause in the action with appropriate comment. Thinking of the unfilial conduct of Haemon they sing about the power of Love, Eros, which can pervert the minds even of the upright. They go on to observe that Eros is a power that ranges through the whole universe—man, animals, gods; Aphrodite sits enthroned beside the Great Powers, and wields absolute sway. Whereupon Antigone is led in, and the action continues.

But if this is the way in which we understand the ode—'Here the Congregation will sing a Hymn'—we have scarcely begun to understand Sophocles. It is true that these reflections on the power of Love are suggested to the chorus by what Haemon has said to his father; it is also true that time after time in this play the chorus says things which are true, but are said about the wrong person—as when in the second ode they speak of the wicked lawbreaker, and in the third ode about evil seeming good to the one whom the god is minded to destroy: in each case they are thinking of Creon's adversary, but in each case it is Creon himself whom the words fit. The two stanzas on Love are not religious poetry written as an interlude by a pious dramatist; they are an important part of the *real* drama. Creon has already defied one part of divine law in refusing burial to a fellow human being; now he defies another of the majestic powers of the Universe in brutally disregarding Haemon's love for Antigone. At this point Sophocles remarks to us: 'Eros, Aphrodite, are gods. They are not to be played with; they are pretty strong. Just wait and see!'—for this is the way in which the ode would be taken by an audience which had not had the advantage of reading books about Greek Tragedy, and was not misled by ideas derived from more romantic kinds of tragic drama.

Accordingly, when this audience heard, later in the play, how the desperate Haemon turned from his lover's dead body upon his father and tried to kill him, and then killed himself, and thus led straight to the suicide of the Queen and the total extinction of Creon's house, it would not say, as we do, 'This is all very exciting, no doubt, but, really, I am much more interested in Antigone than in Creon.' It would say 'What an awful illustration of the folly of a man who presumes to anger a god!'

—H. D. F. Kitto, *Sophocles: Dramatist & Philosopher* (London: Oxford University Press, 1958), pp. 35–37

BERNARD M. W. KNOX ON OEDIPUS' DEATH IN *OEDIPUS AT COLONUS*

[Bernard M. W. Knox (b. 1914) is the director of the Center for Hellenic Studies in Washington, D.C. He has written *Word and Action: Essays on the Ancient Theater* (1979), *The Oldest Dead White European Males and Other Reflections on the Classics* (1993), and *The Heroic Temper* (1964), a study of Sophocles from which the following extract is taken. Here, Knox, seeing *Oedipus at Colonus* as the summation of Sophocles' dramatic work, examines the significance of Oedipus' death in the play.]

The play is a worthy last will and testament. All the great themes of the earlier plays recur; it is as if Sophocles were summing up a lifetime of thought and feeling in this demonic work of his old age. The blind man who sees more clearly than those who have eyes is now not the prophet Tiresias but Oedipus himself, who prophesies, first in the name of Apollo and then in his own. As in the *Oedipus Tyrannus* and *Trachiniae,* the action unrolls against the background of the oracular prophecies of the gods, those cryptic, partial revelations of the divine knowledge which the human intellect cannot accept or understand until they are fulfilled. The heroic creed of Ajax, to reward friends and punish enemies, and that mutability of human fortune which mocks such a creed, reappear in this last play, but with a different emphasis. The theme of the *Philoctetes,* the hero's recompense for unmerited suffering, is used again; like Philoctetes, Oedipus, the despised and rejected, turns out to be the one man his enemies cannot do without, and they come to take him away. And death, that death Ajax and Antigone proudly claimed as their own, which Electra and Oedipus at Thebes wished for in their moments of despair, which Philoctetes preferred to the life among men which he had come, with good reason, to fear—that death is Oedipus' declared goal from the first: he is a wanderer looking for the place where it awaits him, his promised rest.

And the play uses again the familiar situation and formulas of the heroic will and its victory over attempts to turn it aside. This is all the more astonishing because the beginning of the play seems to exclude such a possibility entirely. Oedipus is not only a blind beggar, he is also a very old man. And old men, in Greek tragedy, are not treated too kindly. With the single conspicuous exception of the prophet Tiresias (and even he is treated with a certain measure of cynical irreverence in the *Bacchae* of Euripides), they are always portrayed with a keen eye for the foibles of old age. Officious and complacent like the Corinthian messenger in the *Oedipus Tyrannus,* weak and pathetic like Amphitryon in the *Heracles* or Peleus in the *Andromache,* cynical and selfish like Pheres in the *Alcestis* or Cadmus in the *Bacchae,* garrulous like Tyndareus in the *Orestes,* filled with impotent, bloodthirsty spite like the old servant in the *Ion*—they are usually either slightly ridiculous or sinister. To cast an old man in the role of the hero was a bold step, and of all old men in the world this Oedipus is surely the least likely candidate. When we first see him on stage he is a repulsive sight. His son Polynices describes him for us later. "Dressed in clothes whose old digusting filth has settled on his old man's body, irritating the flesh. On his eyeless head the hair blows uncombed in the wind. And in keeping with all this he carries what appears to be food for his wretched belly" (1258–1263). Sophocles spares us no detail of the hero's sordid condition; it is a salutary reminder, if Philoctetes' unbearable cries of agony did not suffice already, that the modern distinction between Euripidean realism and Sophoclean 'classic restraint' is, like so many such clichés, based not so much on the texts as on an ancient literary tradition which in this case owes more to Aristophanes than to Aristotle.

But this is not all. Not only is the blind, dirty, old man visually an unpromising subject for heroic treatment, he also opens the play with a speech which is total renunciation of the heroic temper: "Who will receive the wanderer Oedipus with paltry gifts today? I ask little and get less, but it is enough for me. I have been taught acquiescence (στέργειν 7) by my sufferings, by my constant companion, long time . . ." (χρόνος 7). "We are come to learn (μανθάνειν 12), strangers from citizens, and to perform what we hear (ἀκούσωμεν 13) from them." This is the mood which all through Sophoclean tragedy the advisors have tried to produce in the heroic soul, acquiescence in the lesson of time. The humility of this speech was not to be expected from the blinded but still demanding Oedipus we saw at the close of the first play. The imperious figure who had to be sharply reminded that he was no longer *tyrannos* in Thebes has with time become humble almost to the point of self-effacement. He is waiting, patiently and in submission, for death.

—Bernard M. W. Knox, *The Heroic Temper: Studies in Sophoclean Tragedy* (Berkeley: University of California Press, 1964), pp. 144–46

G. DEVEREUX ON INCEST AND SELF-BLINDING IN *OEDIPUS THE KING*

[G. Devereux (b. 1908) is a French scholar who has lectured at Temple University, All Souls College, Oxford, and the Ecole des Hautes Etudes en Sciences Sociales, Paris. He is the author of *Dreams in Greek Tragedy* (1976) and *Fantasy and Symbol: Studies in Anthropological Interpretation* (1979). In this extract, Devereux explores the connection between self-blinding and incest in *Oedipus the King*.]

It is proposed to determine whether Oidipous' self-blinding is specifically and primarily linked with his incest, and, if it is, to determine the nature of the nexus between the incest and the self-blinding. The focus of my enquiry is Sophokles' *Oidipous Tyrannos* ⟨S. *OT*⟩, which (except perhaps for Aristophanes, *Frogs* 1195) is the first surviving account of Oidipous' self-blinding. Whether this necessarily means that Oidipous' self-blinding was invented by Sophokles is a problem which does not concern me here.

The first authors to link Oidipous' self-blinding with his incest *only* appear to be Dion Chrysostomos (x 29 f.) and Ailianos (*On the Nature of Animals* iii 47), both of whom deride Oidipous' self-aggression and consider it an insensate or even mad action. Various modern scholars also connect the self-blinding *primarily* with the incest, though already Crusius—probably bearing in mind that punitive mutilations tend to be highly 'crime specific'—noted that self-blinding, viewed as a punishment, does not seem to fit the crime of incest too well. I note in passing that certain variants of this myth, in which Oidipous is blinded by others, link his blinding not with his incest, but with his parricide/regicide.

Freud also appears to have felt that self-blinding, *taken at face value,* was not a very suitable punishment for incest. He therefore interpreted Oidipous' self-blinding as a *symbolic self-castration* in which, through an 'upward displacement', the eyes represent the genitals.

I propose to show that Freud's interpretation of Oidipous' self-blinding as a symbolic self-castration could have been advanced also on purely philological grounds, on the basis of Greek (and Roman) data *only*. However, I must first consider in detail what is said about Oidipous' self-blinding in S. *OT* only.

I begin with a minor matter. Sch. E. *Ph.* 61 ⟨the scholiast on Euripides' *Phoenician Women* 61⟩ asserts that Oidipous was blinded (presumably in S. *OT*) by the curse he himself had hurled at Laios'—at that time still unidentified—murderer. This view implies that even in that case he was blinded *only* because of his parricide, for, when he uttered the curse, Oidipous did *not* know that Laios' murderer was also incestuous. Moreover, his curse does not mention blinding *at all*. As to the Delphic oracle, which *did* know all along the identity and double crime of Oidipous, it spoke only of the slaying or exile of the regicide (100f, 308f.).

One person only—who knew both the identity and the *double* crime of Laios' slayer: the prophet Teiresias—*predicts*

Oidipous' blindness, but does not so much as hint at Oidipous' blinding *himself* (415ff., 454ff.). What matters most is that, *at the time it is made,* Teiresias' prophecy *seems* to predict (somewhat vindictively) this particular calamity chiefly because Oidipous had taunted *him* with his blindness. From the view-point of 'dramatische Technik', it could even be argued that, *at that point,* the audience might interpret Teiresias' prophecy in a figurative sense only. On the other hand, one does note that, on both occasions (415ff., 454ff.) the reference to Oidipous' future blindness is *immediately* followed by remarks concerning his *incest,* which Teiresias is the *first* to mention.

Hence, even though Teiresias' utterances do not clearly and unambiguously mention Oidipous' *self-*blinding, nor explicitly represent his predicted blindness as a *penalty* for his incest, the passages in question are those which come closest to estab-lishing a *basic* nexus between blindness and incest and to indi-cating that the blindness is a punishment or retribution. This inference is materially strengthened by the fact that Teiresias is manifestly unwilling to talk and by the consideration that the utterances of a prophet are necessarily somewhat allusive. In short, Teiresias' remarks are as clear as the dramatic situation and his status as a prophet allow—which is not very clear.

But the authority and nature of Teiresias' utterances also deserve some attention. Though he is angry and offended, his prophecy is *not* a curse; it is simply a prediction: a prophecy. It is, moreover, a prophecy which *differs materially* from what the Delphic oracle prescribes as a penalty for the killer of Laios. That oracle, as we saw, did not mention the incest at all—though it could not but know it—and made not the slightest reference to the blinding of the culprit. In fact, there is little connection between Teiresias on the one hand and Apollon and his oracle on the other hand. Teiresias' prophetic powers come either from Artemis (Callimachus, *Lavacrum Palladis* 121ff.), or from Zeus (Apollodorus iii 6.7)—as do those of Apollon himself (Aeschylus, *Eumenides* 17 f.). Teiresias is a dependent of Apollon only in the very general sense in which all properly authorized prophets are votaries or dependents of Apollon (410).

My next task is to consider in detail Oidipous' own explanations of his deed, which, as will soon become apparent, have certain perplexing features.

Oidipous' explanations require careful scrutiny. One must differentiate between the explanations reported by the Messenger and those uttered by Oidipous himself, on stage. One must take into account the Messenger's state of mind and even more that of Oidipous. Above all, one must carefully appraise the persuasiveness of Oidipous' explanations.

Vv. 1272ff.: Oidipous' statements are selectively reported by a Messenger so upset that he does not even explain what Oidipous meant to do with the sword he had clamoured for (1255). At 1271 he specifies that he mentions only (approximate) samples of Oidipous' statements. At 1289 he explicitly expurgates one of Oidipous' self reproaches. He reports that Oidipous called himself a father-*slayer,* but stops short of repeating *in full* the self-designation: mother-(*defiler*). The fact that, at this point, Oidipous is raving further obscures the meaning of his selectively reported utterances. ⟨. . .⟩

What, then, can be held to have been *explicitly* said? Oidipous accuses his eyes of crimes of commission and omission, which call for punishment—and I hasten to stress that *only* this one of Oidipous' remarks represents the self-blinding as a *punishment.* I note in passing that the sentence construction does not suggest that the visual crime of commission (presumably the sight of Iokaste's nakedness) was worse than the visual sin of omission, nor vice versa. The sin of omission is, needless to say, Oidipous' failure to recognise Laios and/or Iokaste.

—G. Devereux, "The Self-Blinding of Oidipous in Sophokles: Oidipous Tyrannos," Journal of Hellenic Studies 93 (1973): 36–38

[R. P. Winnington-Ingram (1904–1993), a noted British classical scholar, taught at Victoria University in Manchester and the University of London, where he was a fellow of King's College. He wrote *Euripides and Dionysus: An Interpretation of the* Bacchae (1948), *Studies in Aeschylus* (1983), and *Sophocles: An Interpretation* (1980), from which the following extract is taken. Here, Winnington-Ingram discusses the character of Creon in *Antigone,* who is far from being a stereotypical political tyrant.]

Creon is a tyrant—or well on his way to be a tyrant. But he is not the mere stereotype of a tyrant. He is a recognizable human-being, of coarse fibre, commonplace mind, and narrow sympathies. He is a politician without the capacity to be a statesman, because he cannot resist the temptations of power. He is a 'realist', for whom only the visible is real. The range of motives he can understand is limited, including lust for power and greed for money. The fact of death he must accept, but the invisible realm of the dead means nothing to him. He believes in the efficacy of the threat of death: that someone should choose death not in defence of the state but in opposition to the state, not for money but for an emotion and a principle— that is something quite outside his experience and his comprehension. His coarseness of fibre is shown in his disregard of other people's feelings, and notably in his attitude towards Haemon's marriage, since for him one woman is much the same as another—or ought to be; he under-estimates the daemonic power of Haemon's feelings and so loses his son. What does that mean to him? To judge by what he says at 641–7, it was the loss of a utility, of an ally in the battle of friends and enemies. But Creon can never be judged by the straight meaning of what he says, least of all when his words, as so often, are gnomic. Sophocles has an ironic reversal in store for us. When Creon is turned inside out, he is found to be empty (709)— empty of all the principles he has proclaimed. The strong man, who in his obstinacy and self-will had seemed a worthy antagonist to Antigone, collapses. The political man, full of wise saws, who seemed to subordinate all personal relationships to politics, is utterly broken by the loss of a son and a wife. The pasteboard tyrant becomes the most ordinary, if the most unhappy, of men.

The Messenger on his entrance makes this point for Sophocles, who did not waste the seventeen lines of that opening speech (1155–71). As we have already seen, the Messenger's standpoint is that of the average man. When he assumes that chance governs all, he is as wrong as when he denies the possibility of prophecy. Perhaps he may be nearer the mark in his last seven lines, when he reflects upon the downfall of Creon, which he does in terms of pleasure and joy. The theme is insistent (1165, 1170f.). Wealth and power (which had seemed to be the aim of Creon's ambition) he will retain, but joy will be lost, because he has lost his son and, though the Messenger does not know it, will lose his wife. Creon, the political man, in his lust for power, has destroyed his real sources of happiness, which reside in *philoi.* He, not Antigone, ends the play as a 'living corpse' (1167), longing for death but forced to remain in the visible world of life (1332).

—R. P. Winnington-Ingram, *Sophocles: An Interpretation* (Cambridge: Cambridge University Press, 1980), pp. 126–28

DAVID SEALE ON SEEING IN *OEDIPUS AT COLONUS*

[David Seale is the author of *Vision and Stagecraft in Sophocles* (1982), from which the following extract is taken. Here, Seale maintains that the metaphor of seeing is, in spite of Oedipus' blindness, the dominant theme in *Oedipus at Colonus.*]

The idea of seeing is the first and dominant theme of the tragedy: the paradox of blindness and sight is with us from Oedipus' opening to his parting words, the framework of his stage appearance. But it is not simply expressed in the poetic imagery; it is apparent in almost all the stage business, not only in the movements of Oedipus himself but in the arrivals of those he cannot see. The 'eyes' of Oedipus are the image of his whole being, both in its apparent and its real aspects. They are the external emblem of his blindness, of his physical weakness, of his repulsive deformity; they are the essence of his inner vision, of his moral innocence, of his ancient wrath. The whole history of suffering is there in the sightless gaze. The role of Antigone is almost exclusively defined by the blindness of her father. She is his 'eyes'; she is his suffering; she is part of him, a dramatic fact which is well exploited first by the temporary then by the permanent separation. The theatrical impression of an inner world, of Oedipus knowing without seeing all that occurs, resides for the most part in her special function which would be much more effective in performance than can be imagined from the written page.

More than this, every other character is 'discovered' by his own distinctive visualisation of the hero. In this sense the whole of the play is a pattern of response to the *sight* of suffering. The casual piety of the stranger, the superstitiousness of the Chorus, the deep affection of Ismene, the instinctive humanity of Theseus, the suppressed disgust of Creon, the blindness of Polynices, they are all elicited as visual responses to the ruined figure. And, as the introductory element, each visualisation of suffering anticipates the significance of each encounter. In fact, this changing subjective impression of Oedipus dictates the scenic design. The massive intervention of the searching Chorus, between Oedipus' withdrawal into and re-entry from the interior of the grove, structures the drama into a sequence of private and public revelation. Within this basic structure the serene and compassionate insight of Theseus is the immediate preparation for the crafty, then violent, exploitation of Creon and the deluded self-pity of Polynices. And the most hideous visual impression is reserved for the final meeting. Thus the blind delusion of Polynices serves as the dramatic preface to the final display of Oedipus' terrible insight. But the most distinctive feature of the visual design is the symmetry of the two impressive stage movements which, through the transfiguration of the hero himself, sets forth the main development and gives the movement from appearance to reality to formal scenic expression. Both spectacles shine the spotlight on Oedipus himself. For it is in his visual aspect, in the double image of the unseeing and the unsightly, that the essential meaning of the tragedy resides.

—David Seale, *Vision and Stagecraft in Sophocles* (Chicago: University of Chicago Press, 1982), pp. 139–40

RICHARD W. MINADEO ON ANTIGONE'S FLAWS

[Richard W. Minadeo (b. 1929) is a former professor of classics at Wayne State University and the author of *The Lyre of Science: Form and Meaning in Lucretius'* De Rerum Natura (1969), *The Golden Plectrum: Sexual Symbolism in Horace's Odes* (1982), and *The Thematic Sophocles* (1994). In this extract, Minadeo challenges the prevailing view of Antigone's virtuousness by declaring that her words and actions show her to be prideful, self-centered, and full of hatred.]

After failing to secure Ismene's help, Antigone announces that she will bury the body alone; she proceeds alone to the act; even after Ismene is sentenced for the same crime, she behaves as though she alone is accountable; later, she complains against all reality that she is friendless, alone; and she ends by designating herself the lone remnant of her family. The pride in loneliness with which she begins indeed ends in hallucination and regret, but the fact of it remains constant. The word for her state of mind is solipsism, and her solipsism, I suggest, accounts also for her response to the burial that she does not perform. It simply does not exist for her.

In its particulars, the confrontation with Creon only corroborates our main findings, thematic and otherwise, heretofore. The first detail sorely discloses the price of the closeted reading to which the play has been subjected. Having completed his interrogation of the guard, Creon turns to Antigone and says (441),

σὲ δή, σὲ τήν νεύουσαν ἐς πέδον κάρα. . . .
⟨⟨You there, you with your head hanging to the ground. . . .⟩⟩

Sophocles thus injects a rare "stage direction," and if the critics have by and large ignored it, the audience cannot. For Antigone has undoubtedly stood so throughout the guard's long speech (407–439), and must the audience not wonder at her drooping? Jebb, who has, explains that "she is neither afraid nor sullen, but feels that she and Creon can never come to terms." But what has Sophocles to say? Word for word the description of Antigone's posture had been attached to the guards when they realized they must report the first burial to Creon (269f.), and they had hung their heads explicitly in fear.

Does fear also explain Antigone's dejection? I suggest that it does. Tacitly and in miniature we see in her unexpected enervation here a foreshadowing of the loss of nerve she openly displays in her final scene. Now as then the fatal act is done, and the consequences must be faced. Now as then no authentic devotion to principle sustains her. She has gone about the burial because, impelled rather than inspired, she could do no other; and now that the impulse has run its course, she is left drained and, since she does not wish to die, afraid.

It is death that she fears, however, not Creon. Him she loathes and despises as a monster of injustice and the embodiment of her torture. Thus, when addressed with piercing scorn,

> You there, you with your head hanging to the ground,
> do you admit these things or deny them?

she readily summons up a contempt to match. Almost immediately, in fact, she finds herself branding him an abject fool (468f.). Nowhere is her loathing of the man more plainly in evidence.

In the interim she is called upon to justify her daring, and it is here that she voices her exalted appeal to the eternal and unwritten laws of heaven. As blackly as she regards Creon, and here she does not go too far, so splendidly does she gild her own motives. It is her initial dejection, however, coupled with her blaze of scorn which gives us the true measure of Antigone. The dejection is authentic, an *ergon* ⟨act⟩. The appeal to divine law, since, if authentic, it would preclude dejection, is transparent rationalization, sheer *logos* ⟨word⟩. The scornful charge of stupidity, being obviously from the heart, is also *ergon*. It is therefore a fathomless—and, again, not undeserved—personal hatred that enables Antigone to stand up to tyranny, and nothing more sublime.

Sadly, however, she has no capacity for love to match her powers of hatred, a condition which Sophocles now proceeds to expose by means of a crucial nexus of thematic ironies. The discourse turns explicitly to love and hatred, with the theme of sharing stressed throughout. Creon contends that the burial of Polyneices is an affront to Eteocles (522), that "not even in death Is an enemy a friend." Antigone responds with another egregiously admired utterance, "It is not my nature to share in hatred, but in love." She means, of course, that she is barred by nature from joining in Eteocles' hatred for their brother. Winnington-Ingram notes that Antigone has already confuted this claim by invoking Polyneices' hatred against Ismene, which observation alone bleeds the exclamation of all value. Moreover, the verbs *sunechthein* ⟨join in hating⟩ and *sumphilein* ⟨join in loving⟩ do not limit themselves to the suggestion of a shared passion toward a third party. They also signify mutual hatred and love, pure and simple.

On this level Antigone's claim rings ironic to the point of travesty. First, she is at the very moment participating in an orgy of shared hatred with Creon. Compounding the irony, Sophocles brings Ismene instantly onto the scene. She comes shedding "tears of one who loves her sister" (526f.), and her entire purpose is a venture in sharing. She hopes to share her sister's guilt and her fate, in a word, her love, only to find that she remains an object of unremitting hatred by one "born to share in love."

—Richard W. Minadeo, "Characterization and Theme in the
Antigone," Arethusa 18, No. 2 (Fall 1985): 146–48

[Warren J. Lane and Ann M. Lane are professors at the University of California at Santa Cruz. In this extract, the Lanes focus on the "Ode to Man" in *Antigone,* which depicts a model for human political behavior based upon *philia* (friendship).]

The ambiguity of the chorus's final comprehension of what has transpired in Thebes is foreshadowed by the Ode to Man. The ode seems to set out an evolutionary view of political community and the development of the arts attributable to rational mastery of the environment. But at its conclusion this power is seen to be ambiguous at best. The chorus perceive that when human powers lack intelligent moral direction, these capacities and designs recoil and destroy their agents. Although "clever man" subjugates all things on the earth and in the heavens, he may lack proper insight, becoming the victim of his own endowments and achievements, and thus be trapped and overpowered in the "tangled mesh of his nets." There is here an ominous allusion to Creon as the potential victim of his own cunningly contrived loyalty test. But at a more significant level, the words can be understood to introduce Antigone as the genuine embodiment of the daunting though wondrous creature—"man."

In the light of the ode, Antigone's is the eloquent "speech" that amid the silence of the city admonishes those around her. It is her "wind-swift thought" that confronts the crisis created by Creon's ban. She alone thinks and speaks as the guardian of the *philia,* or "feelings that make the town." Not rationalist statecraft (more properly belonging to Creon) but the distinctly non-rationalist, formative impulse of *philia* is identified by the chorus as drawing together and sustaining people and polity.

The ode's concluding lines reinforce this view and focus attention on Antigone. Among all the people of Thebes, and in special contrast to its male citizenry, only Antigone "weaves" into "the laws of the land the gods' sworn right," a genuine concern for loyalty to others—*philia.* Because *philia* is the human element in closest touch with the unwritten, divine law to which mortals are "sworn," only *philia* can keep humans from moral ruin and in touch with honor for self and city.

The ode further elaborates the interlacing of divine and human through the double meaning of those "laws of the land" meant to be leavened by *philia* (369). On one hand, the phrase refers simply to the laws of the polity; but on the other, it identifies the ways of the earth (*chthōn*). The ways of the earth are those of the Erinyes as emissaries of Zeus. His justice governs all things and can be brought into the affairs of the polity only through the promotion of *philia*. The justice-protecting Erinyes always lurk in the background as sanctions for Antigone's acts. Zeus and the Erinyes stand as the guarantors of the quality of workmanship with which *philia* is woven into the fabric of *polis* life. The harsh yoke and harnesses to which Creon turns to organize, or rather confine, political life must give way to the new model for citizenship and rule Antigone represents: the intelligent weaving of firm friendship.

—Warren J. Lane and Ann M. Lane, "The Politics of *Antigone,*" *Greek Tragedy and Political Theory,* ed. J. Peter Euben (Berkeley: University of California Press, 1986), pp. 178–79

SHEILA MURNAGHAN ON ANTIGONE AND MARRIAGE

[Sheila Murnaghan is a professor of classics at the University of Pennsylvania and the author of *Disguise and Recognition in the* Odyssey (1987). In this extract, Murnaghan notes that Antigone's scorn of marriage is in keeping with her temperament and with her position as a woman in the patriarchal society of ancient Greece.]

By stressing ⟨the⟩ institutional aspect of marriage, Antigone places it in the category of those things it is characteristic of her to devalue and reject. For throughout the play she consistently undervalues human institutions. Her conflict with Creon is generated by her tendency to ally herself with what lies outside the realm of human culture—the natural (the blood kinship that ties her to her brother) and the supernatural (the gods whose laws she claims to uphold)—in opposition to the human institutions, most notably the *polis* ⟨city-state⟩, valued by Creon. Thus, she opposes his κήρυγμα or proclamation, a regulation he had contrived in his role as leader of the *polis* with the interests of the *polis* in mind, by reference to a body of laws that, in contrast to the important political institution of the written lawcode, do not depend for their authority or their continuity on the human invention of writing, have no origin or history, can never be changed, and belong not to men but to the gods.

The difference between Creon and Antigone is expressed in a difference of outlook that causes him to stress the political, impersonal dimension of any character or situation while she stresses its personal dimension. Thus they become antagonists because they have different ways of perceiving Polyneices: he chooses to privilege Polyneices' political identity as public enemy of Thebes, while she chooses to privilege his personal identity as her brother. Similarly, Antigone views the family as the locus of intensely-felt personal loyalties while Creon views it in political terms, seeing it, as Knox puts it, as "a sort of training ground for the exercise of political virtue," an arena in which the civic virtues of discipline, obedience and loyalty are to be developed. He identifies service to the family as the exercise of qualities that will allow one to be known as a good citizen: ἐν τοῖς γὰρ οἰκείοισιν ὅστις ἔστ' ἀνὴρ / χρηστός, φανεῖται κἀν πόλει δίκαιος ὤν ⟨He who rules his household worthily will also be seen to be dutiful in the city-state⟩ (666–67). In this he is like Pericles in the funeral oration, who imports an impersonal, political perspective into the family, suggesting that just as a new citizen is as good as an old one from the point of view of the state, so should a new son be as good as an old one from the point of view of his parents.

For Antigone to stress the institutional character of marriage and to dissociate herself from it is furthermore consistent with her gender. It reflects the phenomenon, characteristic of patriarchal societies in which the abstract and the conventional are valued over the natural and are associated primarily with men, that women are relatively less identified with cultural institutions than men. It is also consistent with the actual conditions of classical Athenian society, in which a woman's participation in marriage served primarily to assure the continuity of a household with which she was never fully identified and to provide citizens for a city in which she was never a fully participating member, and in which the role of women in maintaining the *oikos* ⟨household⟩ freed men for cultural and political pursuits from which women were largely excluded. This conception of marriage as an institution allied with the interests of the *polis* and of men is reflected in the *Oresteia,* where, as the complex issues of the first two plays are reduced in the *Eumenides* to a series of sharp polarities, a conflict between ties of blood and ties of marriage becomes identified with a conflict between the interests of women and the interests of men, and with a conflict between the primitive conditions antedating the *polis* and the civilization that the *polis* represents.

—Sheila Murnaghan, "*Antigone* 904–20 and the Institution of Marriage," *American Journal of Philology* 107, No. 2 (Summer 1986): 200–201

MARY WHITLOCK BLUNDELL ON OEDIPUS' MOTIVATIONS IN *OEDIPUS AT COLONUS*

[Mary Whitlock Blundell is a professor of classics at the University of Washington and the author of *Helping Friends and Harming Enemies: A Study in Sophocles and Greek Ethics* (1989), from which the following extract is taken. Here, Blundell shows that the ancient Greek maxim of helping one's friends and harming one's enemies is the basic moral thrust of *Oedipus at Colonus.*]

The twin principles Help Friends and Harm Enemies are fundamental to the structure of *Oedipus at Colonus.* At the outset Oedipus reveals Apollo's prophecy which he wishes to fulfil, and whose fulfilment will constitute the action of the play. He is to find rest at Athens, 'bringing profit by dwelling here to those who welcomed me, but doom to those who sent me away, driving me out' (92f.). The dual theme is restated more explicitly when he tells the chorus that if they help him they will gain 'a great saviour for this city, and troubles for my enemies' (459f.). For the first 700 lines of the play, until Creon arrives, Oedipus' two-edged hopes and emerging power to implement them are constantly stressed. He shows his benign aspect to the Athenians, to whom he promises *soteria* ⟨security⟩ and benefits if they help him (72, 287f., 576–8, 642; cf. 462f., 487). The arrival of Ismene shows his love for his daughters (324–33), and through her message his power over Thebes is revealed (389f., 402). It gradually emerges how he intends to use that power, and the scene culminates in a curse on his sons and a prayer that he may indeed have the control over their fate which the oracle has promised him (421–4). Later, in his long speech to Theseus, it is made clear that the same event will simultaneously bring help to his friends and harm to his foes (621–8), and Theseus' response shows a full understanding of this (635 and especially 646f.).

After the Colonus ode (668–719), which marks Oedipus' full acceptance as an Athenian, the dramatic action polarises the two aspects of the double theme. First Oedipus encounters those natural *philoi* ⟨friends⟩ who have become his enemies, and denounces them with a series of curses of increasing ferocity (787–93, 864–73, 1370–96). This hatred is set in relief by the love between him and his daughters, displayed most intensely after their rescue (1099–1114). When they are restored to him, Oedipus prays gratefully that the gods reward Theseus and Athens as he wishes (1124f.). But it is only after the most terrible curse of all, and Polyneices' tragic exit, that the emphasis switches abruptly to the benign aspect of Oedipus' power. From this moment on he displays both complete confidence that he is following divine guidance, and an urgent desire to reward his friends as he has promised (1489f., 1508f., 1518–55; cf. 1496–8). The prophesied defeat of Thebes is now presented only as a blessing to Athens, not as the destruction of Oedipus' enemies (contrast 621–3). Both here and in the final scene the emphasis is firmly on the beneficial aspect of Oedipus' power.

The whole play is thus stuctured around Oedipus' over-whelming desire and special power to help his friends and harm his enemies. This desire is rooted in the reciprocity of the talio, which he also uses to justify killing his father: 'How am I *kakos* ⟨evil⟩ in my nature? I acted in retaliation for what was done to me, so that even had I done it in full knowledge, not even so would I be *kakos*. But as it is I reached the point I did knowing nothing, whereas those who acted against me tried to destroy me knowingly' (270–4). He extends the right of retali-ation within the family not only to fathers against sons—which is uncontroversial—but also to sons against their fathers, which is quite a different matter. He takes the doctrine of retaliation within the family to its logical conclusion: if striking back is right, why should parents be exempt? Later on, however, he justifies his deed as self-defence against a murderous attack (991–6). Self-defence is retaliation at its most justifiable, and indeed need not to attributed to the talio at all, but Oedipus makes it quite clear that he does consider retaliation just (cf. especially 1381f.; also 868–70).

Creon and Oedipus' sons have forfeited their presumptive *philia*. As Oedipus bitterly tells Creon, 'This "kinship" was in no way *philos* to you *then*' (770f). His sons not only failed to pre-vent his exile, but did not recall him until their own interests were at stake (427–30, 418f., 448f., 599f., 1354–7). Accordingly Polyneices is 'loathed', his voice is *echthistos* ⟨most hateful⟩ and brings great pain (1173f., 1177). He is dis-owned as a son, and a fortiori as a *philos* (1369, 1383). Oedipus reinforces these personal judgements with a thorough moral condemnation. His sons are *kakistoi* ⟨most evil⟩ (418, 1354, 1384), while Creon is *kakos* (783), *kakistos* (866f.), unjust (806f.), irreverent (823), and shameless (863). His daughters, on the other hand, have fulfilled the obligations of kinship-*philia* by subordinating their own immediate pleasure and advantage to his interests. The role of Ismene is ingeni-ously introduced and developed so as to produce a pair of concerned daughters to balance the pair of callous sons (see especially 337–56). They remind us that the sons' behaviour was not inevitable, for even if Oedipus' exile was unavoidable there were ways in which they could have eased his lot. The touching reunion of Ismene with her sister and father, and the mutual affection emphasised after the rescue and at Oedipus' death, make it clear that he is not deficient in *philia* for those children who behave as children ought. He is bound to them by the natural affection of kinship, for as Antigone puts it, 'Everything is *philos* to its parent' (1108). This line is highly ironic in view of the forthcoming confrontation between Oedipus and his son, but it also serves to underline the natural state of family relations which has been perverted by the sons' behaviour. The company of such *philoi* should bring pleasure (cf. 324f.) and delight (cf. 1121f., 1140). After her father's death Antigone realises there is such a thing as 'longing for evils' (1697), and that the non-*philos* can be *philos* (1698), for the pain caused by caring for her father was outweighed by the pleasure of his presence. The messenger reports Oedipus' claim that 'the single word "love" ' is sufficient recompense for all his daughter's hardships (1615–18).

 —Mary Whitlock Blundell, *Helping Friends and Harming Enemies: A Study in Sophocles and Greek Ethics* (Cambridge: Cambridge University Press, 1989), pp. 226–29

CHRISTIANE SOURVINOU-INWOOD ON BURIAL IN *ANTIGONE*

[Christiane Sourvinou-Inwood (b. 1945) is a senior research fellow at Oxford University. She has written *Theseus as Son and Stepson* (1979), *"Reading" Greek Culture* (1991), and *"Reading" Greek Death* (1995). In this extract, Sourvinou-Inwood maintains that it was Creon's failure to bury Polyneices' body at all, not merely his refusal to bury it within the city limits, that is the fundamental moral and religious crime in *Antigone*.]

The play is not saying that Polyneikes should have received proper burial; Teiresias' verdict stresses the disturbance of the cosmic order resulting from keeping a corpse in the upper world. Kreon's mistake lies in the form that he chose to give to Polyneikes' bad death, leaving his corpse exposed. The notion that Polyneikes is entitled to a proper burial is Antigone's position, not the play's. The fact that Polyneikes does get a proper burial does not entail that he was entitled to it at the beginning, and that Antigone's whole position is vindicated. For his achievement of proper burial at this point appears as a corrective excess; Kreon, to repair the wrong done to the gods and the polis, annuls the classification of Polyneikes as traitor and buries him properly, atoning through a complete reversal: from the dishonour and reduction of the corpse to raw food for animals, to a proper optimum burial by, and within, the polis. The standard Athenian modes of ascribing 'bad death' to a corpse did not involve leaving in the world above that which belongs to the gods below. Traitors and temple robbers were denied burial in Attica, optimum burial in and by their community, but were not, in practice, denied burial outside it. When a corpse was thrown out of Attica the presumption was that in reality it would be buried, either by its relatives or by the people of the place who would want to avoid pollution. As for the practice of throwing corpses and/or people as a mode of execution into a pit or a gorge and presumably leaving the corpses there (as, in other states, throwing bodies over a cliff) this would, first, remove the corpses from the areas of human habitation so that pollution was avoided; and second, it would be perceived as symbolically handing them over, down, to the realm of the nether gods. The downwards symbolism would be particularly strong when the bodies (dead or alive) were thrown into pits and gorges. As for those which were thrown into the sea, their mode of disposal reproduced that of many other corpses, of people who had drowned and whose bodies had not been recovered, and this would have made this disposal a symbolically valid mode of handing over the bodies to the nether gods. It is not a matter of 'true' logic, but of symbolic and ritual logic.

On my reading, it is the fact that Kreon kept Polyneikes' corpse in the upper world by not disposing of it at all, *not even symbolically,* that was offensive to the gods, for it blurred the realms of life and death and thus threatened the cosmic order. Sophocles is here exploring the limits of the polis' religious discourse, by presenting one particular articulation of his perception of these limits in one particular area, the disposal of the dead. He locates his exploration in the mythical polis which *par excellence* represents the 'other' in Attic tragedy, and he in turn zooms the exploration towards, and distances it from, Athenian reality, which allows him to articulate the possibility that the polis' religious discourse can unknowingly transgress and offend the gods. The notion that in the *Antigone* Sophocles may be challenging the polis' discourse would be in conflict with what we know both about the reception of *Antigone* and about Sophocles. Sophocles' attitudes helped shape his selections, and are also relevant to the ways in which the fifth century Athenians made sense of the play. Athenian reactions to Sophocles help us see how they understood the play. Far from being perceived as a subversive, a challenger of the values of the polis, Sophocles was a solid citizen who held some important polis offices and was very popular with the judges of the tragedies who awarded him many victories. The story that he was elected general thanks to the success of the *Antigone,* whether or not it had any historical basis, indicates that this play was not perceived as subversive, and that it was felt to be containing the correct attitudes towards the polis.

> —Christiane Sourvinou-Inwood, "Assumptions and the Creation of Meaning: Reading Sophocles' *Antigone," Journal of Hellenic Studies* 109 (1989): 147–48

FREDERICK AHL ON JOCASTA

> [Frederick Ahl (b. 1941) is a professor of classics and chairman of the department at Cornell University. He is the author of *Lucan: An Introduction* (1976) and *Metaformations: Soundplay and Wordplay in Ovid and Other Classical Poets* (1985). In this extract from *Sophocles' Oedipus* (1991), Ahl examines the character of Jocasta in *Oedipus the King.*]

Jocasta asserts herself with confidence the moment she steps on stage. It may seem at first that she separates Creon and

Oedipus as a mother calms an outburst of sibling rivalry. But her language and her authoritative tone suggest rather a judge or magistrate. Note her exchange with Oedipus (698–706):

> Jocasta: Speak—if you'll say precisely on what grounds
> you charge him with beginning this quarrel.
> Oedipus: He claims I'm guilty, I'm Laios' killer.
> Jocasta: He really knows this for himself? Or has he just
> learned about it all from someone else?
> Oedipus: He sent a seer to do his dirty work
> and keeps his own mouth free from all offense.

Jocasta treats the quarrel between Oedipus and Creon as if it were a lawsuit. She carefully distinguishes at the outset between knowledge based on personal familiarity with an incident and information acquired from others, what we would call "hearsay," which was of no account in an Athenian court. At the same time her rhetorical attention is focused not on whether Creon actually said what Oedipus alleges that he said, but on whether Creon was *correct* in the substance of the charges.

Jocasta's questioning is not at all naive. She is leading Oedipus away from any examination of Creon's possible guilt, not exploring it. Indeed, she has already, in a matter of seconds, secured the remission of Oedipus' sentence of death upon her brother. It will not occur to Oedipus again that Creon was (or is) plotting against him.

Jocasta addresses Oedipus as if the real issue were not Creon and conspiracy but Oedipus' personal anxiety that he may be guilty of Laios' murder. And, of course, in a large sense she proves right. She knows Oedipus from years of close familiarity. So too, presumably, do Creon and Teiresias. We, the audience, are just discovering him. We realize in the course of this scene, as we suspected from occasional earlier remarks, that Oedipus is not excluding the possibility that he himself might be the pollution upon the city. Teiresias has, of course, said that the force weighing down on Oedipus is not Creon but Oedipus himself. Jocasta states the matter in legal rather than religious terms: Oedipus is prosecuting himself. She says (707–10):

Well now, acquit yourself of what you've been
saying. Hear me and learn—you should—the proof
that nothing mortal has prophetic skill.
I'll right now reveal signs that show I'm right.

Jocasta in fact pointedly parodies the famous adage about
Delphi: that the god neither speaks nor hides but gives signs.
She herself usurps the oracle's mysticism. And oracular utter-
ances have a special hold on Oedipus' attention.

Jocasta takes it for granted that Oedipus is dissembling when
he claims Teiresias was merely Creon's mouthpiece. She
assumes her husband is frightened by what Teiresias, a
prophet, has said. How much she knows of what the seer proclaimed during his confrontation with Oedipus we cannot tell,
since she was not on stage at the time. Report may have
reached her of what had passed, as it apparently reached
Creon. Has she heard, for instance, that Teiresias proclaimed
Oedipus would discover that he was living incestuously?
Sophocles has drawn an impenetrable curtain here.

—Frederick Ahl, *Sophocles' Oedipus: Evidence and Self-
Conviction* (Ithaca, NY: Cornell University Press, 1991),
pp. 131–33

PIETRO PUCCI ON OEDIPUS AND LAIUS IN *OEDIPUS THE KING*

[Pietro Pucci (b. 1927) is a professor of classics at
Cornell University. Among his works are *Hesiod and
the Language of Poetry* (1977), *The Violence of Pity in
Euripides'* Medea (1980), and *Odysseus Polutropos:
Intertextual Readings in the* Odyssey *and the* Iliad
(1987). In this extract from *Oedipus and the Fabrication
of the Father* (1992), Pucci asserts that the core of
Oedipus the King is the failure, on both a literal and a
metaphorical level, of Oedipus and his father Laius to
recognize each other.]

⟨. . .⟩ Oedipus's ignorance, that is, his incapability of recognizing consciously or unconsciously his father in the man he murders, must be carefully assessed. For indeed what is peculiar and extraordinary in this encounter is that neither father nor son are aware of his reciprocal identity and therefore of his own identity.

This peculiarity may not strike the literal-minded readers who realize that Oedipus and Laius cannot possibly recognize each other simply because they have never met before in their adult life. There is no doubt that this is the literal reason why they do not recognize each other. But the text puts on this empirical fact the investments I am trying to suggest. For if the readers do not take this unrecognizability as an organic condition of the father-son relationship, they will face the predicament of banal and idle questions. They will have to ask themselves questions like: "Why would Oedipus not refrain from killing a man who could just be his father, and in fact, as Jocasta states, looks like him?" Or "Why does he forget the oracle just at this point?" Or "Why does Oedipus marry a woman older than himself?" Unless the readers are ready to interpret Oedipus's relationships with his father and mother as exemplary of the structure that holds them related, they will necessarily have to recognize the implausible nature of the story and of its characters.

The impossibility for the father and the son to recognize themselves as such depends on the fact that what makes a Father is the effect of a metaphysical creation—the teleological force of a narrative that credits him with Father's functions. According to this narrative, which we have tracked in the text, he is the absolute origin, he is the producer of laws, of *nomoi* that are pure in speech and deeds. Insofar as he produces creatures that are identifiable to laws, destinies, and directions, he is a privileged, unique origin and source. This effect marks the Father as a recognizable figure; it grants him a distinctive and unique nature. Glancing at him, we feel that we know what a father is, and that we do not need to add anything to his nature and quality to describe his uniqueness and distinctiveness.

This sort of father figure appeared to us in some divine models—Apollo and Olympus, for instance. Yet, even enthroned in the most sublime metaphysical realm, this father figure does not act as an absolute presence, or as a unique entity. Even in the most edifying descriptions of the divine Father, we have noticed a certain invisibility and absence. Polybus too could not be proved to be Oedipus's *pater*. This absence takes two precise configurations. On the one hand, this father does not himself come to light with his authority and fullness. Apollo reaches his believers only through the voice of his ministers and, even so, this voice is inconsistent and corrupted by chance. Olympus does not seem to stand behind his sons, the pure laws, and seems to the chorus to neglect his father's duty.

On the other hand, the absence of these models of Fatherhood is painfully felt even in the onrush of their *telos* ⟨end⟩, because of some failure of their absoluteness and uniqueness in their act of production and creation. For instance, Zeus, Father of men and gods, is somehow covered and masked by the designation of him as "Olympus" to protect his image from a father/son relationship in which he did not appear as a unique, a pure source. Apollo's absolute distinctiveness as Father of the law gets lost when he appears in bestial attitudes, in violent pursuits, that show him as the mirror image of the son. We have seen that Apollo may be even thought of as the lover of Chance, the father of Oedipus! As these examples come to our mind we begin to feel less sure that we know what a father is. For if he is the mirror image of the son, what does distinguish a father?

If even within this metaphysical realm the Father is marked by some absence, outside it the father is qualified by all sorts of contingent features that essentially bespeak his absence as Father, as the unique being that in its metaphysical ideality we know so well how to define. The father is but a *sperma* ⟨seed⟩ unrecognizable from other *spermata* and, as such, undistinguishable even from his son. In the several figures of the father that the text has offered us, a constant element has surfaced, the mirrorlike relationship of father and son. All the different contingencies that form his figure as a caring, censorial, violent being produce a split and inconsistent figure. In this absence, in this mirrorlike relationship, in these split configurations, the father is of course unrecognizable as a father, that is, in the specific nature and quality that make a father.

As the text presents Oedipus and Laius meeting, looking at each other, and not recognizing themselves, it wants us to understand that the undifferentiated, split figure of the father, this mirrorlike image of the son, has no distinctive, unique qualities and is therefore unrecognizable.

Father and son are unmarked roles unless they relate through a "metaphysical" relation that fills that absence, that unbalances the supplementary relationship between father and son, and that unifies the split figure. But the two characters of the encounter on the Phocal narrow path are perfectly "brothers"— I mean parallel, equal, undifferentiated.

This is the important meaning of the scene as it dramatizes the failure of the two characters, father and son, to recognize each other.

There is an interesting point to be added to this interpretation. Given the nature of the father's and son's relationship as it is elaborated by the text, there would be no reason for Oedipus ever to become aware of his parricide. The law forbidding parrincest has been proleptically presented to him by Apollo, but the god has no power and no concern to forbid his parrincest; he has no presence to prevent appearances and opinions from endorsing perfectly legitimate stories, so persuasive at any rate that they risk mystifying the prophetic *telos*.

In fact, Oedipus's discovery of his patricide remains outside the scope of the oracles, were it not for Teiresias's prophecy that, in Apollo's name, forecasts also the recognition of the murder. What now it takes for the parricide to recognize himself is a trick of chance, which may or may not have the collaboration of the divine *telos:* the arrival of the Corinthian messenger and his disconcerting information about Oedipus's illegitimacy. This recognition will change the father figure and make him distinctive, and the father's murder a crime punishable by the pure laws.

—Pietro Pucci, Oedipus and the Fabrication of the Father
(Baltimore: Johns Hopkins University Press, 1992), pp. 118–21

[Charles Segal (b. 1936) was for many years a professor of classics at Brown University before becoming a professor of classics and comparative literature at Princeton University. He has written many books, including *Tragedy and Civilization: An Interpretation of Sophocles* (1981), *Pindar's Mythmaking* (1986), and *Lucretius on Death and Anxiety* (1990). In this extract from his study of *Oedipus the King* (1993), Segal stresses the greatness of *Oedipus the King* as a quintessential tragedy both in its content and in its form.]

The play is a tragedy not only of destiny but also of personal identity: the search for the origins and meaning of our life, our balance between one and many selves, our recognition of the large areas of darkness about who we really are, and the effort to explore the essential mystery of our selfhood. It dramatizes the lonely path of self-discovery, as Oedipus separates his true self from an illusory self defined by the external status of his kingship, and retraces his existence from powerful ruler to lonely wanderer without parents, city, home, or even a sure name. The hero chosen to perform exceptional deeds has also to undergo exceptional suffering as the polluted parricide and outcast who has infected his city.

Oedipus's story serves as the myth not only of Western personal identity but also of Western cultural identity. In this role he may be paired with the figure of Prometheus in Aeschylus's *Prometheus Bound*. Knowledge in *Oedipus Tyrannus* is the reverse of that in Aeschylus's play, where Prometheus's gift to man is allowing man not to foresee the day of his doom. Prometheus keeps technological man away from knowing his death and thus from contemplating the ultimate meaning of his life. To develop the arts and sciences necessary for the basic needs of society, introspective concerns with identity and ultimate meanings are an obstacle, and a certain degree of metaphysical blindness is an advantage. Hence Prometheus's gift that we not know the day of our death.

Prometheus places us close to the origins of the world; it takes us to beginnings still marked by man's primordial struggle with nature for survival. *Oedipus* describes the tragedy of humanity at a later stage, when a reflective awareness of the world within becomes more important than domination of the world outside. This post-Promethean knowledge is tragic rather than technological; it is a knowledge that looks to ends and ultimate reality rather than to means and immediate goals. Its hero has the fearful task, full of suffering, of unveiling the potential chaos of his world.

At the end of his life, in *Oedipus at Colonus,* Sophocles returns to Oedipus, whom he again characterizes as a paradoxical combination of knowledge, power, and weakness. Now in extreme old age, Oedipus appears as the wandering, defenseless exile from Thebes, a blind and homeless beggar. But he is also the vehicle of mysterious blessings that he will bring to Athens, the city in which he is to be buried and that he will henceforth defend through the magical power of his bones.

Freud saw *Oedipus Tyrannus* as a story of a man's deepest and most hidden sexual and aggressive impulses and made it the founding myth of psychoanalysis. For the general reader today, Oedipus's situation touches another area of anxiety, existential rather than sexual or psychological: the fear of meaninglessness. Oedipus confronts the mystery of being alive in a world that does not correspond to a pattern of order or justice satisfactory to the human mind. He places us in a tragic universe where we have to ask whether the horrible suffering we witness is all due to design or to chance, whether our lives are random or entirely determined. If everything is by accident—a view to which the modern reader is probably more inclined than the ancient one—then life seems absurd. If it is all by design, then the gods seem cruel or unjust, and life is hell. Sophocles does not give a final answer, any more than Shakespeare offers us a final answer for the tragic shape of Hamlet's life or for the death of Cordelia in *King Lear.*

If *Oedipus Tyrannus* is the quintessential tragedy because of its content, it is also the quintessentially classic work in its form. It embodies the "classic" in its combination of intensely powerful emotions contained in an austere, controlled structure. Both plot structure and language operate within a severe economy that is both dense and lucid. The rhythm of Oedipus's search and discovery has no equal in theater. The bits of information come naturally, randomly, and yet inevitably, and we watch with horror as Oedipus is forced to the terrible conclusion. Every detail, virtually every sentence, contributes to the dramatic effect, and nothing seems superfluous. The language is powerful in its immediate context but often carries a double or triple meaning.

Sophocles' play asks, Why do our lives turn out to have the shape that they finally have? He opens before us a kaleidoscopic configuration of different possibilities: the circumstances of our birth, our character, parental nurture or its absence, sheer luck, a mistake or miscalculation or wrong decision at a crucial moment, a mysterious doom or destiny, will of the gods. Over the centuries readers and audiences have found different answers and emphasized different aspects of the play. There is so much in Sophocles' dense weaving of the simple and the complex that, as the classicist and translator Richmond Lattimore wrote, "We can read *Oedipus* as many times as we like, and every time find new truths and throw away old falsehoods that once seemed to be true. There is always a dimension that escapes."

—Charles Segal, Oedipus Tyrannus: *Tragic Heroism and the Limits of Knowledge* (New York: Twayne, 1993), pp. 13–15

Books by Sophocles

Greek text:

Tragaediae [*sic*] *Septem cum Commentariis.* Ed. Aldus Manutius. 1502.

Tragoediae Septem. Ed. C. G. A. Erfurdt. 1802. 7 vols.

Tragoedien. Ed. Gottlieb Carl Wilhelm Schneider. 1824–37. 10 vols.

Tragoediae. Ed. Eduard Wunder. 1831–37. 2 vols. in 7.

Tragoediae. Ed. Wilhelm Dindorf. 1832–36. 3 vols.

Sophocles. Ed. F. W. Schneidewin. 1855–58. 6 vols.

The Plays and Fragments. Ed. R. C. Jebb. 1883–96. 7 vols. (with English translation).

Sophocles. Ed. F. Storr. 1912–13. 2 vols. (with English translation).

Fabulae. Ed. A. C. Pearson. 1924.

Sophocle. Ed. Alphonse Dain. 1955–60. 3 vols. (with French translation by Paul Mazon).

Tragoediae. Ed. R. D. Dawe. 1975–79. 2 vols.

Oedipus Rex. Ed. R. D. Dawe. 1982.

Antigone. Ed. Andrew Brown. 1987 (with English translation).

L'Oedipe roi de Sophocle. Ed. Jean Bollack. 1990. 4 vols. (with French translation).

English translations:

Oedipus, King of Thebes. Tr. Lewis Theobald. 1715.

The Tragedies of Sophocles. Tr. George Adams. 1729. 2 vols.

The Tragedies of Sophocles. Tr. Thomas Francklin. 1758–59. 2 vols.

Tragedies (Oxford Translation). Ed. Theodore Alois Buckley. 1823. 2 vols. in 1.

Tragedies and Fragments. Tr. E. H. Plumptre. 1865.

The Seven Plays. Tr. Lewis Campbell. 1883.

Sophocles in English Verse. Tr. Arthur S. Way. 1909–14. 2 vols.

Oedipus, King of Thebes. Tr. Gilbert Murray. 1911.

King Oedipus. Tr. W. B. Yeats. 1928.

The Antigone of Sophocles. Tr. Dudley Fitts and Robert Fitzgerald. 1939.

The Antigone. Tr. Gilbert Murray. 1941.

Oedipus at Colonus. Tr. Robert Fitzgerald. 1941.

The Theban Plays. Tr. E. F. Watling. 1947.

Oedipus at Colonus. Tr. Gilbert Murray. 1948.

Oedipus Rex. Tr. Robert Fitzgerald. 1949.

Sophocles. Tr. David Grene, Robert Fitzgerald, Elizabeth Wyckoff, John Moore, and Michael Jameson. 1954–57. 2 vols.

Three Tragedies: Antigone, Oedipus the King, Electra. Tr. H. D. F. Kitto. 1962.

Oedipus Tyrannus. Tr. Luci Bekowitz and Theodore F. Brunner. 1970.

Oedipus the King. Tr. Anthony Burgess. 1972.

Antigone. Tr. Richard Emil Braun. 1973.

Oedipus the King. Tr. Stephen Berg and Diskin Clay. 1978.

Oedipus the King. Tr. Robert Bragg. 1982.

The Three Theban Plays. Tr. C. A. Trypanis. 1986.

Works about Sophocles and the Oedipus Plays

Bloom, Harold, ed. *Sophocles.* New York: Chelsea House, 1990.

―――― ed. *Sophocles'* Oedipus Rex. New York: Chelsea House, 1988.

Burton, R. W. B. *The Chorus in Sophocles' Tragedies.* Oxford: Clarendon Press, 1980.

Bushnell, Rebecca W. *Prophesying Tragedy: Sign and Voice in Sophocles' Theban Plays.* Ithaca, NY: Cornell University Press, 1988.

Cameron, Alister. *The Identity of Oedipus the King: Five Essays on the* Oedipus Tyrannos. New York: New York University Press, 1968.

Champlain, M. W. "*Oedipus Tyrannos* and the Problem of Knowledge." *Classical Journal* 64 (1968–69): 337–45.

Dimock, G. E. "Oedipus: The Religious Issue." *Hudson Review* 21 (1968–69): 430–56.

Dyson, M. "Oracle, Edict and Curse in *Oedipus Tyrannos.*" *Classical Quarterly* 23 (1973): 202–12.

Ehrenberg, Victor. *Sophocles and Pericles.* Oxford: Basil Blackwell, 1954.

Fortes, Meyer. *Oedipus and Job in West African Religion.* Cambridge: Cambridge University Press, 1959.

Gellie, George. *Sophocles: A Reading.* Melbourne: Melbourne University Press, 1972.

Golden, Lester M. "Freud's Oedipus: Its Mythos-Dramatic Basis." *American Imago* 24 (1967): 271–82.

Green, André. *The Tragic Effect: The Oedipus Complex.* Tr. A. Sheridan. Cambridge: Cambridge University Press, 1979.

Grene, David. *Reality and the Heroic Pattern: Last Plays of Ibsen, Shakespeare, and Sophocles.* Chicago: University of Chicago Press, 1967.

Harsh, P. W. "Implicit and Explicit in the *Oedipus Tyrannos.*" *American Journal of Philology* 79 (1958): 243–58.

Hester, D. A. "Oedipus and Jonah." *Proceedings of the Cambridge Philological Society* 23 (1977): 32–64.

Hoey, Thomas. "On the Theme of Introversion in the *Oedipus Rex.*" *Classical Journal* 64 (1968–69): 296–99.

Hogan, James C. *A Commentary on the Plays of Sophocles.* Carbondale: Southern Illinois University Press, 1991.

Howe, Thalia Philies. "Taboo in the Oedipus Theme." *Transactions of the American Philological Society* 93 (1962): 124–43.

Kane, Robert L. "Prophecy and Perception in the *Oedipus Rex.*" *Transactions of the American Philological Association* 105 (1975): 189–208.

Kaufmann, Walter. "Sophocles: The Poet of Heroic Despair." In Kaufmann's *Tragedy and Philosophy.* Garden City, NY: Doubleday, 1969.

Keddie, J. N. "Justice in Sophocles's *Oedipus Tyrannos.*" *Antichthon* 10 (1976): 25–34.

Kitto, H. D. F. *Poesis: Structure and Thought.* Berkeley: University of California Press, 1966.

Knox, Bernard M. W. *Oedipus at Thebes.* New Haven: Yale University Press, 1957.

Lattimore, Richard. *The Poetry of Greek Tragedy.* Baltimore: Johns Hopkins Press, 1958.

Lattimore, Steven. "Oedipus and Teiresias." *California Studies in Classical Antiquity* 8 (1975): 105–11.

Lenieks, Valdis. "The Foot of Oidipous." *Classical World* 69 (1975): 35–44.

Lesky, Albin. *Greek Tragedy.* New York: Barnes & Noble, 1965.

Lloyd-Jones, Hugh. *The Justice of Zeus.* Berkeley: University of California Press, 1971, pp. 104–28.

McDevitt, A. S. "Dramatic Imagery in the Parodos of the *Oedipus Tyrannos.*" *Wiener Studien* 4 (1970): 28–38.

Margon, Joseph S. "Aristotle and the Irrational and Improbable Elements in *Oedipus Rex.*" *Classical World* 70 (1976): 249–55.

Melchinger, Siegfried. *Sophocles.* Tr. David S. Scrase. New York: Ungar, 1974.

Moorhouse, A. C. *The Syntax of Sophocles.* Leiden: E. J. Brill, 1982.

Musurillo, Herbert. *The Light and the Darkness: Studies in the Dramatic Poetry of Sophocles.* Leiden: E. J. Brill, 1967.

Paolucci, Anne. "The Oracles Are Dumb or Cheat: A Study of the Meaning of *Oedipus Rex.*" *Classical Journal* 58 (1963): 85–101.

Peradotto, John J. "Oedipus and Erichthonius." *Arethusa* 10 (1977): 85–101.

Rado, Charles. "*Oedipus the King:* An Interpretation." *Psychoanalytic Review* 43 (1956): 228–34.

Rigsby, K. J. "Teiresias as Magus in *Oedipus Rex.*" *Greek, Roman and Byzantine Studies* 17 (1976): 109–14.

Rosenmeyer, Thomas G. "The Wrath of Oedipus." *Phoenix* 6 (1952): 92–112.

Rudnytsky, Peter. *Freud and Sophocles.* New York: Columbia University Press, 1987.

Scodel, Ruth. *Sophocles.* Boston: Twayne, 1984.

Segal, Charles. *Tragedy and Civilization: An Interpretation of Sophocles.* Cambridge, MA: Harvard University Press, 1981.

Sewall, Richard B. *The Vision of Tragedy.* New Haven: Yale University Press, 1959, 25–43.

Stewart, Harold. "Jocasta's Crimes." *International Journal of Psychoanalysis* 42 (1961): 42–30.

Sutton, Dana F. *The Lost Sophocles.* Lanham, MD: University Press of America, 1984.

Tonelli, Franco. *Sophocles' Oedipus and the Tale of the Theatre.* Ravenna, Italy: Longo, 1983.

Van der Sterren, H. A. "The *King Oedipus* of Sophocles." *International Journal of Psychoanalysis* 33 (1952): 343–50.

Vellacott, Philip. *Sophocles and Oedipus: A Study of the* Oedipus Tyrannos. London: Macmillan Press, 1971.

Vernant, Jean-Pierre. "From Oedipus to Periander: Lameness, Tyranny, Incest in Legend and History." *Arethusa* 15 (1982): 19–38.

Vickers, Brian. *Towards Greek Tragedy.* London: Longman, 1973.

Waldock, A. J. A. *Sophocles the Dramatist.* Cambridge: Cambridge University Press, 1951.

Weil, H. S. "Oedipus Rex: The Oracles and the Action." *Texas Studies in Literature and Language* 10 (1968): 337–48.

Index of
Themes and Ideas

Mount Laurel Library
100 Walt Whitman Avenue
Mt. Laurel, N.J. 08054-9539
(609) 234-7319